40 Days in the

Wilderness

Meditations for African American Men

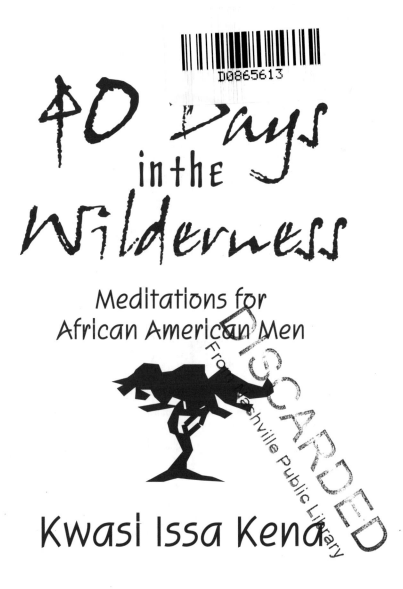

Kwasi Issa Kena

ABINGDON PRESS

Nashville

Property of
The Public Library of Nashville and Davidson County
225 Polk Ave., Nashville, Tn. 37203

D0865613

DISCARDED

From Nashville Public Library

FORTY DAYS IN THE WILDERNESS:
MEDITATIONS FOR AFRICAN AMERICAN MEN

Copyright © 1998 by Abingdon Press

All rights reserved.

No part of this work may be reproduced or transmitted in any form or by any means, electronic or mechanical, including photocopying and recording, or by any information storage or retrieval system, except as may be expressly permitted by the 1976 Copyright Act or in writing from the publisher. Requests for permission should be addressed in writing to Abingdon Press, P.O. Box 801, 201 Eighth Avenue South, Nashville, TN 37202-0801.

This book is printed on acid-free paper.

ISBN 0-687-071801

Unless otherwise noted, Scripture quotations are taken from the HOLY BIBLE: NEW INTERNATIONAL VERSION ®. Copyright © 1973, 1978, 1984 by the International Bible Society. Used by permission of Zondervan Publishing House. All rights reserved.

Scripture quotations noted KJV are from the King James Version.

Those noted TLB are from The Living Bible. Copyright © 1971 by Tyndale House Publishers. Used by permission.

Those noted NRSV are from The New Revised Standard Version Bible. Copyright © 1989 by The Division of Christian Education of The National Council of the Churches of Christ in the United States of America. Used by permission.

98 99 00 01 02 03 04 05 06 07—10 9 8 7 6 5 4 3 2 1

MANUFACTURED IN THE UNITED STATES OF AMERICA

To my sons, Tony and Chris, and to my nephew

Chris Wise—young men being shaped by the wilder-

ness experience. May God grant you unending

strength for the journey.

Contents

Acknowledgments

No book is ever written alone. This book of meditations is no exception. It is the result of multiple influences, loving support, and divine inspiration. First, I thank the Lord Jesus Christ for impressing me with the desire and inspiration to write. I also am grateful for my parents, William and Alicia Bishop, for providing a lifetime of support and encouragement. I appreciate my sister, Patrice Bishop-Wise, for sharing her timely and wise advice.

Apart from the Lord, my greatest motivation to write came from my wife, the Reverend Dr. A. Safiyah Fosua. Her tireless support, keen insights, and loving assurance made writing this book a most pleasurable experience. I thank her for reading, re-reading, editing, and sharing in the birth of this project.

Next, I am indebted to the men who helped shape a wholesome image of manhood before me.

To my father, William Bishop, and my late grandfather John Hal Bishop (Gramps), whose consistent examples provided me with a firm foundation of manhood.

To my grandfather "Bud"—whom I knew only through the memories of my mother, Alicia Bishop, and my late grandmother Nettie Simpson (Grandmama)—for his calm nature and sense of humor.

To my other "fathers":

Mr. Tremerell Hunter, who instilled in me the confidence to do things that I thought were impossible.

Mr. John David, who demonstrated the value of living a life of integrity before a young developing teenager.

Mr. Tony King, who taught me cultural pride and excellence in the arts.

The Reverend Walter Goodlette, who exemplified the "joy of the Lord" and the excitement of teaching the Bible.

The Reverend G. Calvin McCutcheon (Pop), my "father in the ministry," who allowed me to grow under his grace and wisdom.

To my uncles: George Rogers, William Simpson, George Simpson, and the late Pat Goggans, each of whom took time to nurture me in invaluable ways.

To my best friends in the world: Ron Barker, Jr., and Keith Childress, who know me and still love me. They supply me with much needed doses of "brother love."

To my pastor/friend, the Reverend Dr. C. Anthony Muse, of Resurrection Prayer Ministries in Brandywine, Maryland; my brother in Christ, who loves the Lord greatly and inspires me to do likewise.

To my mentors, Dr. Jeremiah Wright, Jr., of Trinity United Church of Christ in Chicago, and Dr. Jawanza Kunjufu of African-American Images, who inspired me to explore and discover a cultural and intellectual depth for the purpose of leading the next generation.

To James (Jimmie) and Louise (Lou) Porter, and the staff and directors of KBBG Radio, Waterloo, Iowa, who gave me the opportunity to try my hand at devotional writing through early morning radio devotions.

To Dr. Delano "Kim" Cox, Duane Moorehead, the Reverend Charles Miller, and Mickey Johnson; the Jubilee United Methodist Church Men's group which helped forge ideas of manhood development.

To Dr. Kofi Duodu and Forster Kwame Boateng and their families, who have become my family in Ghana. To all of those who took the time to read samples of this manuscript and offered helpful feedback: Mrs. Judy Baity, Leron Rogers, Joe Tendai Mucherrera, Tengeni Shiimi-ya-Shiimi, Rheta Smart (MaRheta), the Reverend Dave Markay (General Board of Global Ministries missionary in Lithuania), and the Reverend Don Hamilton (General Board of Global Ministries missionary in Zambia).

To the countless men of this and past generations who have helped to shape within me a healthy manhood image.

Introduction

The wilderness: bleak, desolate, isolated. No one desires the wilderness; yet, none of us can avoid our predestined encounter with it. Life thrusts us into the wilderness for a variety of reasons. Moses escaped into the wilderness. Paul sought refuge in the wilderness. The Spirit of God drove Jesus into the wilderness. A place frequented by so many of God's chosen servants deserves closer attention. What is so essential about this inevitable experience?

In each situation, the men in the wilderness had a face-to-face encounter with God, unhindered by the distractions of familiar surroundings. People become disoriented in the wilderness. This seems to be God's intent. When placed in situations where our normal coping mechanisms fail, we must turn to the God who is greater than any problem.

African American men especially need the wilderness. Each day society bombards our psyche with unyielding challenges to our cultural, relational, and spiritual selves. Healing and perspective can come only when we decide to create our own spaces for prayer and reflection. Historically, our spirituality as Africans and African Americans has served as a guidepost through life. Spirituality stands as a sanctuary of sanity. Now, more than ever, we, as a spiritual people, must take time to examine who we are in the mirror of God's Word. This book, written for African American men, serves as a catalyst for honest reflection, purposeful meditation, and noticeable transformation.

The wilderness is the place of transformation. Moses entered, fearing for his life. He entertained notions of liberating his people from bondage, but he had no feasible means of accomplishing it. His ways were not God's ways. We are no different. That's why God challenges the human spirit to change.

In the wilderness, God provokes us to greatness, toughens us to withstand temptation, and calls forth our hidden potential. In the wilderness, the Lord enlarges our vision to include his perspective of life. In the wilderness, the Holy Spirit strips away baggage too heavy for us to carry through the next stage of our lives.

Moses returned from the wilderness to lead Israel from Egyptian bondage. Paul emerged from the wilderness to spread the gospel to the Gentile world. Jesus left the wilderness to embark upon his miraculous earthly ministry. You too can rise from the wilderness to pursue your God-given destiny. New beginnings, new discoveries, renewed strength, and revitalized lives result from meeting with God, alone, in the wilderness. Can you afford to miss your appointment there?

Transformation doesn't come quickly or easily, though. Your encounter with God must be long enough to bring about permanent change—thus forty days in the wilderness. The number forty represents an important time span throughout the Bible. Noah experienced rain for forty days. Moses spent forty days in the presence of God on Mt. Sinai. God fed the Hebrews with manna for forty years in the wilderness. The number forty must represent a time period that is long enough for God to get his point across to an individual or to a nation.

Your forty-day journey may take many forms. You may choose to travel alone, reflecting on the Scriptures, stories, and prayers provided for each day. Each selection includes the section "For Further Meditation," which is designed to help you put a spiritual principle into practice using prayer, questions for reflection, or a spiritual exercise.

Others of you may decide to walk with fellow "journeymen." (A "journeyman," as defined by James E. Kilgore in *The Intimate Man* [Nashville: Abingdon Press, 1984], is one who has knowledge and skills, yet is open to learning new ways based on experience. He has moved beyond the apprentice stage but is not yet a master craftsman. He is on a journey to find a new way of life. Says Kilgore, "The men we call journeymen are no longer imprisoned by rigid notions of how males are supposed to behave or respond. Instead they are exploring new and creative solutions to situations and challenges in their day-to-day living.")

This book is appropriate for use in Sunday school classes, in men's groups, in retreat settings, or as a Lenten exercise. Your private or group devotions will have their greatest impact only if you are determined to be honest with yourself and with God.

As you choose to travel into the wilderness, remember that it is a place of personal discovery, spiritual encounter, and divine purpose for the future. Don't get cold feet. The Lord will be with you every step of the way. He will provide everything you need to complete the journey. Remember, two helpings of "angel food" sustained Elijah for forty days at Mt. Horeb (1 Kings 19:4-8).

For some, the wilderness is a place of endless wandering. For others, it is a place of ceaseless discovery. You decide. Why not be the determined soul who dares to fulfill your divine destiny? Journey now with God for forty days in the wilderness.

Day 1
Forty Days in the Wilderness

At once the Spirit sent [Jesus] out into the desert, and he was in the desert forty days, being tempted by Satan. He was with the wild animals, and angels attended him.

—Mark 1:12-13

Jesus had just been baptized, marking the beginning of his earthly ministry. This should have been a mountaintop experience, leaving him nowhere to go but up. Instead, the Spirit drove him out into the wilderness.

Have you ever felt that you were pushed "out there," alone in the wilderness? Some men experience the wilderness when they reach the milestone years: thirty, forty, fifty, or sixty years of age. These ages are times of evaluation in a man's life. By now, we reason, we are supposed to have "made something of ourselves." We begin adding up our achievements and assets to see how we have fared in the game of life.

A lot of soul searching goes on in the wilderness. We examine every conceivable angle. *I could have tried harder here. I should have gotten a break there. Maybe I've just been wasting my time.* We sometimes can be our own worst enemies.

Before you follow a similar path, take time to reexamine today's passage. Notice, it was the *Spirit of God* that sent Jesus into the wilderness for forty days, where he was tempted by Satan. The Son of God endured the wilderness to clearly establish the grounds upon which he would live his life. The circumstances facing Jesus were not pleasant, but through it all God was with him. Scripture says the angels were also there attending to him.

I suspect God still sends men into the wilderness for spiritual preparation. Perhaps God sends us there to drive us away from the pursuit of our humanly constructed goals. Once we allow our grasping hands to release what we think is best, we can discover what God knows is better. What is your life based upon? Is your striving in vain? Are you in a rut? Maybe this is your wilderness. Stop struggling for a moment and listen to what God is trying to say to you.

When we are finally exhausted from self-condemnation and hopeless delusions, we are able to hear God speaking words of life to our haggard souls. We then learn that our manhood is not measured by whether or not we acquire the fictional American Dream. Our self-worth clearly comes from whether we base our lives on God's Word.

When we finally submit to God's intentions for our lives, those troubling temptations to be like "so and so" lose their appeal. We find that establishing a strong spiritual foundation weakens the voice of temptation.

Make no mistake: the wilderness is tough. The wilderness is a time of stripping away part of our old "self." It's a time of being alone with God. If we dare to go through it honestly, however, we'll be the men that God wants us to be—full of integrity, motivated by the Spirit of God, and ready to be godly examples in the world.

FOR FURTHER MEDITATION

Prayer

Lord, the wilderness is a place for personal transformation. It is a place for repentance, restoration, and redirection. In solitude, there is time for reflection. I need the wilderness. Give me the courage to face each moment in the wilderness with honesty and openness. I am determined to emerge from this experience as a man changed for the better. Lead me by your guiding Spirit. Amen.

Day 2

My Father
My Friend

"Then the master called the servant in. 'You wicked servant,'
he said, 'I canceled all that debt of yours because you begged
me to. Shouldn't you have had mercy on your fellow servant
just as I had on you?'"

—Matthew 18:32-33

Why does that boy always mess up? Sidney wondered to himself. "Ronnie!" he shouted. "Can't you stay out of trouble for more than two minutes?"

Fourteen-year-old Ronnie just breathed and stared in response. There are times when the demands of fatherhood challenge your every waking moment. For Sidney, things became tense when Ronnie became a teenager.

Ronnie seemed troubled about a lot of things lately. Confusion clouded his mind about school, about women, about being a man, about living at home. But like most fourteen-year-olds, he couldn't figure out what really was bothering him.

Sidney looked disgustedly at Ronnie's things scattered across the living room. Clearing away the debris, Sidney plopped in front of the VCR and put in a video for some mindless activity. Before long, his mind drifted into a dreamy state of half-sleep. Without realizing it, today eased into Sidney's past.

Sidney was once young with more energy than sense.

Flashes of his youthful escapades pierced his thoughts. His mind raced to the time when he and his friend Thelonious tried to buy something "in a little brown bag," while they were underage. Next, his memories reminded him of the fact that his own son, Ronnie, was conceived because he and Sarah had gotten "too friendly" in his cousin's basement. Like a swollen river, Sidney's past flooded his mind. His memories became a reflecting pool of instruction.

Scattered words from the Sunday sermon drew his situation into perspective: "Since God's mercy is as bountiful as a Thanksgiving dinner, why can't we learn to offer a scrap of forgiveness to each other?" A chill raced down Sidney's back. God's grace had picked him up after many falls. But Sidney had never taken time to honestly share his life experiences with his son. How is Ronnie ever going to learn how to *live* if I never share my life with him? he wondered.

Sidney's own father, "Papa," was also very private about his personal life. Papa made it clear that he was "The Man," an authority to be respected without question. Unfortunately, that meant that Sidney wrestled with hundreds of unvoiced questions alone, without the benefit of Papa's insight.

Papa believed that children were to speak only when spoken to. He seemed to believe that if Sidney managed enough "yes sirs" and stayed out of trouble, mature manhood would somehow come. Sidney's behaviors toward Ronnie had become a reflection of Papa's influence. It was only recently that he and Papa were able to share more than "polite talk." Each conversation watered Sidney's thirst for a "father-friend." What could have happened if these talks had come sooner?

Now Sidney faced the same communication problems with his son. *If I'm not careful, Ronnie's life is going to be a reflection of my youth,* he thought. Fragments of Sunday's sermon hung in his mind. "Lord," he prayed, "if you can have patience with me, I can have patience with Ronnie."

"Ronnie! Ronnie! Come here for a minute. I want to tell you about some things that used to happen to me when I was your age...."

FOR FURTHER MEDITATION

Prayer

Dear Lord, help me to see my life as a gift to be shared with others. Teach me the value of leading young boys into manhood and maturity. Amen.

The Next Step

1. While you were growing up, how often were you engaged in honest, transparent dialogue with your: father, mother, other family members, friends?

2. Do you honestly share your life experiences with your children and/or with other youth who may learn from them?

3. Is transparent dialogue a regular part of conversations in your home?

Day 3
The Belly God

For, as I have often told you before and now say again even with tears, many live as enemies of the cross of Christ. Their destiny is destruction, their god is their stomach, and their glory is in their shame. Their mind is on earthly things.
—Philippians 3:18-19

Man, you just got to know how to *train* a woman. You 'The Man!' She got to do what you say do!"

Willis had his new coworkers mesmerized with his well-worn speech. Sensing that he had a fresh audience, he cleared his throat and started rehearsing *what real men do*.

"See, in my house, I'm in control from jumpstreet. In the morning, Beulah knows she got to have my eggs easy, my toast buttered, my bacon crisp, and my coffee hot by 5:45 A.M. One time she tried to say she was feeling bad and wanted me to eat some instant oatmeal. Man, I like' ta knocked her into tomorrow's sunrise! She only tried that mess with me one or two more times.

"Now when I get home at night, she knows she better have my supper hot and ready. And I don't mean no warmed-up yesterday's food. I like everything fresh, today-made. See, my mama always made something fresh for my daddy *and* had something sweet for dessert, too. I like cobblers, you know—peach or blackberry.

Either that or a 'tata pie with ice cream on the side—not on top, on the side. I can't stand to have my ice cream melt all over my hot pie.

"You young brothers need to learn how to run yo' house. Most of y'all don't know nothin' about what I'm talkin' 'bout. Ain't too many men around no more. Most of y'all got to ask your wife to blow your own nose...."

Across town, Beulah stared at the phone for the third time this morning. Finally, she picked it up and called Mariah, her best friend.

"Girl, how you doing? Me? Oh...I don't know. I ain't been able to sleep much lately. Nerves, I guess. I'm not sure what's wrong, but even my hair is starting to fall out. My stomach's in knots all the time, and I just don't feel like doing much at all. Me and Willis? Oh, we're okay...."

Beulah deftly turned the conversation toward a less intrusive area. She wanted—needed—to talk to somebody about her marital friction, but she was taught not to air any dirty laundry.

When she hung up the phone, she tearfully reflected on the promises Willis had made when they were dating. "Baby," he had said, "you need a man to take care of you. I'll treat you right, all day, all night. See, me and you, we can make it."

For better, for worse...
For richer, for poorer...
In sickness, and in health...
Till death do us part...
I DO!

Just then the sound of Willis's ten-year-old "deuce and a quarter" brought her back to reality. Tears welled up in her eyes and fear churned in her stomach as she smelled the stench of dinner burning. She had committed the cardinal sin: failing to offer an acceptable sacrifice to the god of Willis's belly. His shrill whistle knifed through the air, announcing his arrival at the back door. Immediately Willis noticed the foul odor.

"Aw naw, I know that ain't my supper burning!" he bellowed from the doorway. Beulah just sat—motionless. Only the outer shell of her "self" remained. Her soul had long since died...

For a crust of bread...
A piece of meat...
And a cool drink....
Was it worth it?

FOR FURTHER MEDITATION

Prayer

Dear Lord, forgive me for placing so much importance on my selfish wants. Show me the joy that comes from unselfish living. Amen.

The Next Step

1. Did you notice any similarities between Willis's behaviors or attitudes and any of your behaviors or attitudes?

2. Do you regularly participate in meal preparation in your home? *Helping with the process builds greater appreciation for the meals served in the home.*

3. If someone observed you near supper time, would it appear that you love food more than people?

Spiritual Exercise

Consider fasting from time to time. Instead of eating a meal, use that time to be considerate to your family. For more insights on fasting, read Isaiah 58.

Day 4
Liquid Language

As he approached Jerusalem and saw the city, he wept over it.
—Luke 19:41

I t will be all right. Your mama's in a better place now. She wouldn't want you to be sad now. She gave you all she had to give, and now we've got to make her proud of us."

Michael dryly mouthed those borrowed words to his children. The premature death of his wife threw his family into a numbing melancholy. His hollow words fell lifelessly to the ground. Like an overused funeral script, his attempt at consolation failed to convince himself or his children. The words he spoke didn't reflect his true feelings.

Michael's mind swirled with rage and anger, pity and grief, sorrow and anguish, abandonment and loneliness. But his face betrayed none of these emotions. Like a stone flint, Michael set his jaw and toughed out the Friday night visitation. He stood at the door, shaking everyone's hand and thanking them for coming. Porter, Shaneel, and Tijuana, his three children, melted into his lap after everyone left.

"What are we going to do? Mama's gone...."

Tears gushed from their eyes. Michael just stared into an empty corner as if looking for some diversion from his children's pleas.

On the morning of the funeral, Michael braced himself for the worst day of his life. Relatives from all over the country were there. His wife, Bobbie, had been the family favorite. She had a smile that could light up a thousand midnights. Her laugh was contagious and her cooking superb. She was everybody's sister or mama or friend. She was his lover, his companion, his best friend. *How could God do this to me?* he thought. *We were barely together ten years!*

At the church, the funeral seemed to drag on forever. Everybody had a poem or a special song or a resolution for the church archives. When Reverend Maxwell got up to preach, he gathered his thoughts around one theme— the compassion of Christ. Masterfully, he painted a portrait of Jesus as one who lived a life of compassion and deep passion for others. "Because of Jesus' example," he said, "we don't have to be afraid of loving too much or grieving too hard...."

Michael's nerves began to tingle. A mist appeared in his eyes. A tear tried to force its way out of the corner of his eye. This was no easy task. Michael's rigid self-control rarely allowed public displays of emotion. He didn't cry when they took his father's withered body to exist in the nursing home. He didn't cry when his sister lost her first child. He didn't cry when they first diagnosed Bobbie's cancer.

He didn't cry...

He couldn't cry...

He wouldn't cry....

A glance at Bobbie's lifeless body reminded him that she was gone. Just then, a persistent tear pushed past his defenses. Exhausted from decades of keeping vigil, Michael's self-control finally collapsed. One tear followed another until a steady stream dug pathways down his cheeks. He sat statue-still; only his tears moved. Each salty drop released his pent-up compassion for his wife. With one loud cry, Michael stood and wept loudly in the middle of Reverend Maxwell's sermon. Immediately, he felt loving arms of compassion around his shoulders and three sets of arms around his knees.

There are some things that words cannot express. For those things, God gives us a liquid language. Compassion and healing flowed from Michael's heart that day, thanks to the strength of his tears.

FOR FURTHER MEDITATION

Prayer

Dear Lord, emotions are sometimes new and frightening to me. I want to be strong. Show me the depth of strength needed to express the full range of my emotions. Teach me the value of being genuine. Help me to discover the powerful compassion revealed in Jesus Christ. Amen.

Day 5

Whose Report Do You Believe?

Finally, brethren, whatsoever things are true, whatsoever things are honest, whatsoever things are just, whatsoever things are pure, whatsoever things are lovely, whatsoever things are of good report; if there be any virtue, and if there be any praise, think on these things.

—Philippians 4:8 KJV

Sticks and stones may break my bones, but words—they can kill you.

Since our arrival, they have said:

You're three-fifths of a human being.

You're genetically inferior.

You evolved from the lesser-intelligent apes. No amount of civilizing will ever make you fully human.

You can only sing, dance, and run fast...so entertain me.

I'm sorry. Your kind is not allowed in here.

You must be mistaken; that apartment is already taken.

I would charge my own brother the same price for this car.

You're overqualified for this job. Sorry.

Police brutality? Look! He was resisting arrest!

Sorry. Your credit history's not strong enough.

You don't look like a lawyer. Try a trade school.

Our economy cannot support Haitian immigrants.

Apartheid was an insufficient reason to become directly involved in their internal affairs.

Reparations for slavery are just not feasible.

Social pressures? No! Your hypertension is probably due to a genetic deficiency.

Color has nothing to do with my decision.

You've got to admit: things are getting better for your people.

Why, some of my best friends are Black.

Our voices join the chorus, saying:

Slavery was good; it brought us Christianity.

My Sunday school teacher says we're messed up 'cuz of some curse of Ham.

We can't run nothin' but a barbershop and a barbecue shack.

You think you're something 'cuz you got a college degree.

I got mine; you got yours to get.

She ain't no good; all a "sister" wants is your money.

You ain't nothin', and you ain't never gonna be nothin'.

I should'a known I couldn't trust him.

I'm just dealing until I get my money straight.

I carry this piece to make people respect me.

I'm not hooked; I can stop anytime.

You know, Mama always said a Black man ain't worth nothin'.

But, since Creation you have said:

"What is man that you are mindful of him, the son of man that you care for him? You made him a little lower than the heavenly beings and crowned him with glory and honor. You made him ruler over the works of your hands; you put everything under his feet" (Psalm 8:4-6).

FOR FURTHER MEDITATION

Prayer

Lord, I choose to silence the clamor of earthly voices. I choose to believe heaven's report. With your Spirit I soar and confess that I am wonderfully and fearfully made. I live my life as a "hallelujah anyhow"! Amen.

The Next Step

1. Whose voices have the greatest influence on your life?

2. Do you find yourself spending a lot of time attempting to disprove the stereotypes that exist about Black men?

3. How much influence do you honestly allow God to have in your life?

Day 6

"Lord, You Know..."

Another angel, who had a golden censer, came and stood at the altar. He was given much incense to offer, with the prayers of all the saints, on the golden altar before the throne.
—Revelation 8:3

What do men's prayers look like when they get to heaven? Can't you see them? Many prayers stumble through heaven's gates like lost vagabonds, because they don't get out often. They mull around, gazing at heaven's great mansions, and have to be prodded into revealing their purpose for coming. Once they remember their mission, our prayers clear their throats and begin to rattle off their reason for approaching God.

A few of our prayers have problems mustering up the courage to speak. Some come with hat in hand because years have passed since their last visit. Others carry thick keloid scars inflicted while chasing worldly pleasures. Still others stand wondering how to explain their last set of broken promises.

Old-timer prayers push the newcomers aside and take the lead. Religious prayers spout off vain clichés before unimpressed angels. Angry prayers spray and fizzle like a warm, agitated cola. Grieving prayers writhe and ooze like slow molasses. Sneaky prayers glance over their shoulders, hoping no one at home saw them leave.

What do your prayers look like?

God, help me.
   I promise to do better.
      Teach that boy something quick!
         We can't keep living like this!
            God, when?
               Lord, how long?
                  Jesus, why?

No matter the condition of our prayers upon their arrival, God is glad to hear from us. The angels take our fledgling prayers and douse them thoroughly with much incense. Dressed in fragrant clothes, our prayers ascend acceptably to God's throne.

In reality, there is no need to feel awkward about approaching God with our prayers. God already knows our condition before we think to pray. God knows our embarrassments. God knows our frustrations. God knows our deepest needs. God knows and invites us to come boldly into his presence.

Did you pray today? If it has been a long time, start by saying, "Lord, you know...."

FOR FURTHER MEDITATION

Prayer

Dear Lord, today I am encouraged to pray more often to you. I know that you will take my prayers and look past my words until you discover my intentions. Thank you for always desiring to hear from me. Amen.

Spiritual Exercises

1. Write down three or more pressing concerns. Offer them to God in prayer and look for a response from

God. (Note: God's response may be a sense of relief, actual solutions, new discoveries, or changes within yourself or others.)

2. Read one chapter in Psalms and one chapter in Proverbs daily as part of your prayer devotion to God.

Day 7
Indispensable!

But in fact God has arranged the parts in the body, every one of them, just as he wanted them to be.... The eye cannot say to the hand, "I don't need you!" And the head cannot say to the feet, "I don't need you!"
—1 Corinthians 12:18, 21

The Black woman has long pioneered, preserved, and prodded our race forward. She rose in full stature, as Harriet Tubman, to lead us out of slavery. She stood immovable, as Mary McLeod Bethune, to educate our future. She sat determined, as Rosa Parks, in a seat she had every right to. She ran for office to prove it possible, as Shirley Chisholm, presidential candidate. She spoke and shook the nation, as Barbara Jordan, Democratic keynote address speaker.

When segregation and racism scoured the South, she was able to get "day work" when he couldn't get any work. We don't know how many times she was mistreated, propositioned, belittled, and humiliated while going to and from work. She wouldn't tell—she couldn't tell—for fear that her man would retaliate and be jailed or beaten or lynched. She learned to fight with mother wit, and to maneuver with her mind to gain victory where fists failed. Today she flies into outer space, heads major corporations, and preaches God's Word.

Our women are God-given jewels, sparkling with grace, sharpened with determination, chiseled with endurance, and polished with resiliency. Black women are catalysts for success. No need to be jealous.

Those parts of the body that seem to be weaker are indispensable (1 Corinthians 12:22*b*).

Be inspired and add to the blessings she started. Sing songs of encouragement and cooperation. Let history record our hearty "amen" to her achievements. Rise up, Black man, in that call-and-response style that characterizes our music and sermons, and say, "Thank God for the Black woman."

The parts that we think are less honorable we treat with special honor (1 Corinthians 12:23*a*).

FOR FURTHER MEDITATION

Prayer

Dear Lord, give me the courage to regularly encourage and compliment Black women. Help me to begin with those closest to me. Push me past any awkwardness or embarrassment. Disarm attitudes of competition, jealousy, or superiority that I may have developed toward women. Show me the great rewards that come from partnership with our precious women of ebony hue. Amen.

The Next Step

1. How often do you encourage Black women?
2. Do you feel awkward about sharing compliments with them? Why or why not?
3. Go out of your way to become an encourager in your family, work place, church, and community.

Spiritual Exercise

Pray regularly for your wife—or, if you don't have a wife, for your sister or cousin or niece—to fulfill her dreams and aspirations in life. Take an active part in helping her achieve her dreams.

Day 8

Gramps's Peach Cobbler and Daddy's Chili

I long to see you so that I may impart to you some spiritual gift to make you strong—that is, that you and I may be mutually encouraged by each other's faith.

—Romans 1:11-12

Grandson: Ooooooh, what's that?

Grandfather: Peach cobbler.

Grandson: Gramps, is that the only kind of pie you know how to make?

Grandfather: You don't have to eat it if you don't like it.

Grandson: Naw. That's okay. I like peach cobbler, but how come you don't ever make any other kind of pie?

After that, my face would disappear while I devoured two or three helpings of Gramps's syrupy sweet peach cobbler—you know, the kind that makes you gulp down a glass of milk to keep from overloading your pancreas with sugar. Nobody made cobbler like Gramps did.

Father: Put some more chili powder in there...and some salt. Now. All right. Did you put some tomatoes in it? You've got to have tomatoes....

Son (to himself): I thought I knew how to make some chili. Why do we need so much stuff in here? I thought it was just some meat, some beans, and a little spice. This thing is getting pretty involved.

Father: Did you put any onion in there?

Son: No...

Father: Put some onion in there, too...

I didn't realize it at the time, but these were spiritual gifts that my grandfather and my father were passing on to me. As the family recipes passed from generation to generation, part of the enormous strength of my forefathers transferred to me.

Something akin to a spiritual transfusion results from each entanglement with these memories from the past. They help guide my future. No, peach cobbler and homemade chili won't get me a job or pay my bills. But the character and the personality of the men who accompany those memories inspire me to live up to my potential. Their personalities rise to erect an honorable standard for me to follow.

Africans believe that people never completely die until they are forgotten. Memories lure us into a sacred world where our souls can be renewed and reconciled with the past. The more I age, the more I long for more memories, more glimpses of the past—my past. In a time of rediscovering Black manhood, memories of my ancestors are like manna to my hungry heart.

Memories yank the past into the present to influence the future. If you embrace them, memories can become as dear friends and "journeymen" through life's twisted pathways.

I never got to know Granddaddy "Bud." He died the year I was born. I choose to call him Granddaddy Bud, although I don't know what kind of grandfather name he would have liked to be called. Still, I know him in a way—through stories, the memories of my late grandmother, and my mother. They told me about "Bud" (Grandmama's pet name for him). From their stories, his patience, wisdom, and sense of humor became living influences on my being.

Shared memories lift the veil of the past that too easily falls when our loved ones die. Does anyone lift the veil for you in your family? Are there stories lying dormant that need telling?

Memories are markers of the past and makers of the future. Granddaddy Bud's patience and Gramps's cobbler are more precious now than when those men physically walked the earth. Daddy's chili tastes even better now, because we're physically separated by an ocean and six time zones. But memories never die. They seem to take on a life of their own.

I have heard that cousin Kenny now makes peach cobbler just like Gramps did. Who knows how many memories will mark, mold, and make our lives.

Pass me some more of that peach cobbler, please. . . .

FOR FURTHER MEDITATION

Prayer

Dear heavenly Father, teach me about manhood through the memories of my elders. Help me to imitate their most admirable qualities. Mold me by your hand. Make me into a man worthy of being remembered by others. Amen.

The Next Step

1. Feelings of support, acceptance, and direction arise when we share experiences with others. What kinds of experiences do you share with others?

2. Mentoring is playing the role of a journeyman who accompanies another. The time you share with others, especially your children and other youth, is a vital step in the mentoring process. Who is benefiting from your life experiences?

3. Pray for guidance about what to share and to whom to be a mentor in life's journey.

Day 9
"Hush!"

They rushed over and woke him up. "Master, Master, we are sinking!" they screamed. So he spoke to the storm: "Quiet down," he said, and the wind and waves subsided and all was calm! Then he asked them, "Where is your faith?" And they were filled with awe and fear of him and said to one another, "Who is this man, that even the winds and waves obey him?"
—*Luke 8:24-25 TLB*

This must have been a savage storm. The disciples were not unfamiliar with high winds and churning. What was it about this storm that struck fear into their hearts? Was it the sight of the vicious waves crashing over them? Or, was it the sound of impending danger? Perhaps they heard the wood creaking and straining under the power of the surf. Or, maybe the sound of their own noisy fears struck panic inside their hearts. The inward noises of their minds drowned the voice of faith that Jesus had been nurturing within them.

NOISE! Unorganized sound. Uninvited intrusions. Unruly decibels bombarding everything in their pathway. Life is full of noisy trespassers. How many of us are familiar with the following scene?

Gerald opened his front door and greeted his friends. Without warning, the chest-thumping sounds of his monster mega-bass system collided with the tranquil evening air. Once inside, Brandon, Tyrone, and Julian made their way into the living room. There, the TV was blaring the pregame highlights. Gerald motioned for his friends to sit down while he switched channels with the remote and finished talking to LaWanda on the phone.

"What's up, fellas?" Gerald said, smiling with an infectious grin. For the next hour, the four friends tried to carry on a conversation, watch the game, and talk to their other friends on the phone.

Constant exposure to noise can lull you into believing that this should be your normal, accepted routine. Constant noise creates the illusion of activity and purpose. We only become concerned when the storms of life blow in unexpected noises.

The windstorm surprised the disciples. These were frightening noises for them. They feared for their lives and called on the Master to save them. Jesus turned to the waves and said, "Quiet down." One translation simply has him saying, "Hush!" (Mark 4:39a Goodspeed). Then Jesus turned to the disciples and asked them a curious question: "Where is your faith?" Somewhere in their walk with Jesus, the disciples had failed to learn how to exercise faith in God when it really counted.

Perhaps the noises of the day, the noises of their minds, the noises of distraction, had lured the disciples away from listening to Jesus. When noise is the norm, we often stop looking for quiet places where we can hear God.

How much noise surrounds your day? Can you imagine how often we strangle God's voice with the constant sounds that consume us? I have to believe that the disciples' problems began long before they got on the boat and encountered the winds and waves. They had the

Master with them daily and still failed to listen to him. Jesus is just as close to us today, but we seem to cry out to him only when the unexpected storms of life threaten us.

How much effort do you make to create some quiet time to hear what God has to say to you? Perhaps it's time to have a word with the noise that you create in your life: all-day music, TV, telephone, computer, and your own voice—"shooting the breeze," fussing, and complaining. Be bold enough to face the noise and say, "Hush! I need some quiet time with the Lord." You may discover a faith that will anchor you in the storms of life.

Shhhhhh. Listen. The Lord may be speaking right now.

FOR FURTHER MEDITATION

Prayer

Lord, forgive me for shutting you out with the constant noises in my life. Teach me to value moments of silence with you and with myself. Amen.

Spiritual Exercises

1. Create quiet spaces for yourself this week.
Suggestions:

a. Turn off your car radio/cassette while driving to or from work.

b. Turn off the TV an hour early before retiring for the evening, and spend that time with the Lord.

c. Rise a little earlier and take a quiet walk or ride to begin your day with God.

2. Refuse to allow noise to dominate your life and cheat you out of meaningful dialogue with God.

Day 10
Caught in the Act

He came as a witness to testify concerning that light, so that through him all men might believe.

—John 1:7

Star athletes often loom larger than life to us. Jordan and Magic, Bonds and Griffey, Rice and Emmitt—a single name stirs up memories of their legendary feats. Some of yesterday's stars deserve equal billing. Before the age of multimillion-dollar contracts, there stood an athlete who showed his greatness off the playing field. The story is told of Billy Bruton, star center fielder of the then Milwaukee Braves.

Bruton emerged as one of Milwaukee's favorite ballplayers after hitting a game-winning home run in the tenth inning of the Braves' first home game of the 1953 season. He led the National League in stolen bases for three consecutive seasons, and became one of six players to lead off a World Series game with a home run. But his true stardom occurred off the playing field.

Bruton and Bob Allen, his agent for baseball memorabilia and card shows, once shared a motel room during a promotional tour. Exhausted from a long day, his agent politely said good night and started off to sleep. Instead of following a similar path, Bruton focused on something more important than much-needed rest. Before he dozed off, Allen saw Bruton kneeling at the side of his bed, praying. Not knowing what else to do, Allen got on his knees, too. When Bruton finished, Allen asked him what that was about.

"I'll tell you, Bob" he said. "You know, when I was a kid I was a really good baseball player, and thought it would really be something to play in the big leagues. But I knew I couldn't. Now I play in the big leagues next to Henry Aaron and behind Warren Spahn, and make a fine living.... Every night I get down on my knees and thank God for being so good to me and my family" ("Former Brave Bruton Dies," Daniel P. Hanley, Jr., *Milwaukee Journal Sentinel*, December 6, 1995).

Jesus left us in charge of Christian recruitment. We never know how our lives may have an impact on other people. Real spirituality never goes off duty for the night. Our Christian lives are God's constant witnesses to others. Through our lives, other men and women can come to Christ. Let your spiritual light shine. You never know when you may be "caught in the act."

FOR FURTHER MEDITATION

Prayer

Dear Lord, I pray that my Christian lifestyle will be a constant witness for you—even behind closed doors. Amen.

Day 11

Where Are You Headed?

When he saw the crowds, he had compassion on them, because they were harassed and helpless, like sheep without a shepherd.

—*Matthew 9:36*

Being from the city, I had never noticed it before, but after living in Ghana for several months it became very apparent: sheep and goats are extra dumb. One day we were riding with Kwame, one of our Ghanaian friends, in the capital city of Accra. Out of the corner of my eye I spotted a long-legged goat turning its head to look at something across the road. Undaunted by the stream of 60 mph traffic, the goat began crossing the divided highway. In seconds the goat was upon us. "Look out!" I yelled. Without breaking stride, the determined goat plunged headlong into the side of our jeep. I turned around and watched the goat hobble to the side of the road. "Well," Kwame said matter-of-factly, "he will die."

Now that I've started driving in Ghana, when I encounter a goat or sheep I take special notice of which direction their heads are turned. If their heads are turned away from the road, there is no concern. But if their heads are pointing toward the road, I put my foot on the brake. At any moment, these thoughtless creatures may decide to munch on a morsel "over there." Once that little fury head is aimed in your direction, no amount of screeching tires, blowing horns, or shouting voices can deter him. Watch out, he's headed this way! Once a determined leader of the herd starts, the rest follow—danger or no danger. Are we much different?

While I was attending Bradley University in the seventies, the Reverend C. T. Vivian came and delivered a pointed speech to our Black student body. In a dynamic address, he prodded us to direct our lives with meaning and dignity. "What's your perspective?" he echoed again and again. I still remember the impact of his question on my thinking.

In later years, a dynamic revival preacher came to my home church in Milwaukee and addressed the youth. "When we were growing up, we marched and fought for civil rights," he intoned. "We all knew what direction we needed to take. But when I look at your generation, I'm left confused. What is your purpose? What is your purpose?" His words challenged our indecisiveness.

From time to time, we need people to prod us, prick our consciences, and poke our priorities. Many of the victories won during the Civil Rights Era are now reversed. Where are we headed? Black-on-Black crime persists in epidemic proportion. Where are we headed? During "The Movement" years, Black women were *most comfortable* meeting a "brother" on the streets. Today, Black women are *most frightened* to meet a Black male on the corner. Where are we headed?

A million of us marched on Washington in 1997, looking for direction. So many of us don't know who we are. We're bankrupt culturally. We're impotent spiritually. Too many of us face life without God's guidance.

Jesus' words have haunting relevance today: "They were harassed and helpless, like sheep without a shepherd." Without a shepherd, sheep are destined to headlong destruction. Without the Lord, we're headed for trouble. Life has a way of blowing horns, shouting warnings, and allowing near accidents when we wander from God and good sense. Listen closely. Maybe God is asking you the question: Where are you headed?

FOR FURTHER MEDITATION

Prayer

Dear Lord, I submit myself to your divine guidance. Without your direction, my life wanders aimlessly. Focus my priorities on activities with purpose and significance. Help me to serve the cause of Christ and my community. Amen.

The Next Step

1. How would you summarize your main purpose in life? If you don't know how to answer that question, earnestly ask God to reveal the answer to you.

2. What role does God currently play in the direction of your life?

3. Who benefits when you fulfill your purpose for living? Yourself? Others? Our culture? In what ways do you and/or they benefit?

4. Take time to examine where you are headed:

a. spiritually

b. culturally

Day 12

Shifting Gears

The glory of young men is their strength, gray hair the splendor of the old.

—*Proverbs 20:29*

Boyhood fantasies drive many of us—even as adults. Do you remember watching the fluid movements of Cane from the television series *Kung Fu*? Did you imitate every flying kick you ever saw Bruce Lee do? How many unknowing friends fell prey to one of your newly learned YMCA judo moves? Even today some of us jump at the thought of learning capoeira, a Brazilian martial art form with African roots.

What is it about superior power, strength, and ability that intrigues us? True enough, there is a gratifying sense of accomplishment that comes from "benching" 250 pounds, breaking a board, or earning a belt. Our self-confidence erupts each time we achieve anything athletically. That should be no surprise. Scripture points out that "the glory of young men is their strength."

The second part of that verse, however, is equally important: "Gray hair [is] the splendor of the old." The onset of gray hair signals to us the time to shift our confidence from physical strength to wisdom. How many weekend warriors still try to prove their youthfulness by "playing some ball" with broken-down knees, long-neglected muscles, and under-conditioned hearts? Isn't it about time to make a transition from youth to wise man? The youthful feeling of invincibility that comes from athletic prowess is short-lived glory. There comes a time in all of our lives when we must reevaluate that which defines us. As our physical strength fades, we should focus on the eternal strength present in God through the Holy Spirit.

Through the ages, wise men have discovered a deeper strength and satisfaction when they have begun to spend more time with God. They have made a conscious shift in focus from physical strength to God-centered strength.

"God is our refuge and strength, an ever-present help in trouble" (Psalm 46:1).

Have you taken time to consider the depth of God's power? Today is a good day to start shifting your gears.

FOR FURTHER MEDITATION

Prayer

Dear Lord, I understand that my body will weaken with age. Your Word tells me that wisdom now should be my pursuit. With your help, my spirit can grow wiser and stronger with each passing day. Redirect my attention to discover your wisdom. I submit myself to your guidance. Amen.

The Next Step

1. Memorize Psalm 46:1 and repeat it daily for one week as a means of consciously redefining your strength.

2. Consider "retiring" from those sports that do you more harm than good. Replace them with physical activities that promote endurance, good health, and longevity.

A Real Superman

That is why, for Christ's sake, I delight in weaknesses, in insults, in hardships, in persecutions, in difficulties. For when I am weak, then I am strong.

—2 Corinthians 12:10

an, you're tougher than Bo Jackson and Deion Sanders put together," his friends would say. No one doubted that Rashad was pro material. From all appearances, he had everything going for him. He starred in both football and baseball. Going into his senior year of college, the news media labeled him as a shoo-in for the Heisman. The Yankees were ready to sign him to a multiyear contract that would make him the richest rookie in the history of baseball.

Rashad knew his potential, and maintained his competitive physique through a rigorous weight-training program. On campus, everyone hailed him as "Superman" because nothing seemed impossible to him. Who could have anticipated what happened next.

Rashad left his apartment to put in a couple of miles on the cross-country course. He stretched, checked his watch, and started his morning training ritual. Jimmy, the track captain, caught up to him after about a half mile.

"Hey, Rashad, want to run some sprints?" Jimmy asked.

Rashad was never one to pass up an opportunity to test his athletic prowess. "When?" he asked.

"Now," said Jimmy, bolting ahead.

Rashad raced forward to catch him. After thirty yards, they were running neck and neck.

Then it happened: Rashad's foot found a gopher hole; his left leg twisted under him, and he heard a hideous crack from within his body. He fell down, screaming in pain.

"Jimmy, Jimmy, help me, man!"

Jimmy thought he was joking. "You can't fool me with that one; I got you this time."

Rashad cried out again. "Jimmy, I'm hurt, man. Call an ambulance."

This time Jimmy knew Rashad was serious.

In ten minutes the ambulance arrived and rushed Rashad to the emergency room. The doctors took X rays and worked on him throughout the morning. Finally they gave him a sedative and some painkillers. When Rashad woke up, the doctor stood over him, reviewing his chart.

"Doc," Rashad asked, "how long am I gonna be out?"

"Well, that depends on what you're talking about. You'll be released from the hospital tomorrow, and you can attend classes as well. But I'm afraid your days as a serious athlete are over. You had a freak accident that left you with a severely torn ACL, a sprained ankle, and a hip pointer. Your knee will never be able to endure the pounding of professional sports."

It must have been three o'clock in the morning before Rashad finally fell asleep. His whole career vanished in one split second. He replayed the scene a hundred times in his mind. Each time he mentally tried to sidestep the gopher hole, but the outcome was always the same.

The next morning his father, an accomplished musician and businessman, called from Ohio. "Hello, Rashad. I heard what happened, son. How are you feeling?" Rashad answered his father's questions mechanically for the next five minutes. Finally, his father began to reason with him.

"Look, Rashad, every athlete knows that he runs the risk of severe injury every time he plays or practices. When you signed up for that athletic scholarship, we talked about preparing you for life, not just the pros. It looks like you'll have to concentrate on life preparation now.

"Look, son, tragedy doesn't have to end greatness. Quincy Jones was well on his way to becoming a 'monster' jazz trumpet player and composer when tragedy struck his life. Before he had the chance to fully develop his potential, he suffered a devastating brain aneurysm. He, like you, had to make a career adjustment.

"Rashad, you can spend the rest of your life grieving the loss of a career you never had, or you can choose to refocus your greatness. Quincy did, and he became one of the most versatile and creative geniuses that the music industry has ever seen.

"What about you? Are you going to be like so many other college stars who end up gazing through a beer bottle, trying to relive the glory days? Or, are you going to discover that there is strength in the midst of apparent weakness? Don't tell me you're going to let one hardship stop you from being successful in life. I know this is the toughest thing you've ever had to face, but you can do it."

Rashad's father knew how to challenge his son's resiliency.

"Rashad, God gave you a good brain; use it. Find another area to excel in, and make yourself proud."

Rashad thanked his dad and hung up the phone. After

a week of moping, he called his school advisor to discuss changing his major.

Prayer

Dear Lord, release me from endlessly replaying the unchangeable past. Show me instead your view of my purpose and potential in this life. Amen.

The Next Step

1. Think of the most challenging hardships you have faced in life. Did you choose to allow them to strengthen you or weaken you?

2. *Reframing* is a counseling term that invites a person to look at an old situation in new ways. Look at some disturbing past experience and "reframe it" in a positive light.

Day 14
Honest with God

"Before I formed you in the womb I knew you, before you were born I set you apart...."

—*Jeremiah 1:5*a

Harold slid over to make room for an elderly lady to sit next to him on the bus. She plopped down, fiddled with her shopping bag, readjusted her flop hat, and cleaned her glasses before finally feeling a little settled. After a while, Harold's new traveling companion grunted as she reached down to pick up her pocketbook. With weatherworn arthritic fingers, she opened her purse and pulled out a daily devotional booklet: "A Word for Today." It was the same devotional his grandmother used to read every morning.

Harold reminisced about the times when he used to visit her. Before they could eat breakfast in the morning, his grandmother would read out loud the devotion's title, the scripture, the story, and the prayer. (When Harold was old enough, she made him do all the reading.) Then, just when Harold would be ready to stab a spicy piece of sausage, his grandmother would preach a while and urge him to pay attention. She had a time getting Harold to listen, because his mind was on those scrambled eggs, butter biscuits, and homemade preserves staring him in the face. His grandmother would conclude her sermonettes by saying,

"Harold, you can't fool God. He knows everything; so don't ever be 'shamed to tell him what's on your mind. You'll feel better when you do. Are you listening to me?"

It's funny that his grandmother's words came back to him at that moment. Harold was in the midst of some intensive soul searching. At his job, things were getting complicated. Harold worked in accounting. He was always good at making sense out of numbers. His accounting teachers always said he could see more things in a few numbers than most folks could get out of a book. That's why it was so disturbing when Harold began to see some questionable figures occurring in the monthly income statements. Something wasn't right. It looked like the company was projecting greater income than it actually generated.

When he approached the chief accountant about it, Harold was promptly told to do his job and crunch numbers, that he was "the new kid on the block" who didn't quite understand the company's system of accounting its assets. For weeks, Harold tried to ignore the conflict within his conscience.

His problems at work were complicating things in his marriage as well. Each time Harold lost himself in thought, his wife, Melissa, would ask if anything was wrong. Harold, who prided himself on solving his own problems, gave Melissa every superficial answer in the book. Finally, Melissa pressed him, saying, "Look, I'm your wife, and I know you. Something's wrong; you're not acting like yourself. Stop playing with me and talk." That's when Harold exploded: "You just think you know me. Give me some space and I'll be just fine. I don't need everybody crawling around in my head, trying to tell me what I'm thinking."

That was enough to start the worst argument of their two-year marriage. Melissa picked up the car keys and said, "Fine, I'll leave you alone with yourself. Have a good time." That's why Harold found himself on the bus that morning.

"'Scuse me, young man, would you mind if I sit near the window? The light over there is better for reading."

Harold's traveling companion startled him back to reality. He moved to the other side of the seat and continued to think. *Well, Grandma,* he thought, *you always said the Lord knows everything. I hope he can help me know what to do.*

In seconds, the events of work and home blurred as Harold became more engrossed in his conversation with God. In a strange, awkward way, Harold found himself confessing to God that he was confused, angry, hurt, and sorry about the whole situation. "God," he prayed, "what am I going to do? I need a job, but I can't keep ignoring these lying numbers. Besides, now I'm starting to lie to my wife to cover the lies at work. We've never had this kind of argument before."

Harold drifted between talking to God and trying to work out his problem in his own mind. Finally, he sighed and said, "God, you've got to show me what to do, because I don't know."

In moments, Harold heard the word *integrity* sounding in his mind. Somehow, he knew that he had to make a solid decision about living a life of integrity and honesty at home and at work—regardless of the price. Without any flashes of lightning or pounding thunder, Harold realized that God had answered him. It wasn't an easy answer, but it was the right answer.

Well, Grandma, Harold thought, *you were right. It pays to be honest with God.*

FOR FURTHER MEDITATION

Prayer

Dear Lord, I am reminded today that you see and know all about me and my circumstances. Help me to be a man of godly integrity before you and the world. Amen.

Day 15
Church!

See to it, brothers, that none of you has a sinful, unbelieving heart that turns away from the living God.
—Hebrews 3:12

They ain't worth nothin'...none of 'em! Every preacha' I know is either chasin' skirts or milkin' members for money. It's a racket. You can't tell me nothin' good about no preacha'. I tell you what, I ain't gonna have my woman up at that church-house every time it opens...not with that slick pretty-boy preacha'. There ain't *that* much to do at church anyway."

Have you ever heard, thought, or spoken these words? There's a strange, distrustful relationship that exists between some Black men and Black male preachers. Sadly, the criticisms are not always unfounded, and cannot be quickly dismissed. Nevertheless, the preacher is not your problem.

If your spouse or significant other is drawn to the house of worship, which so many Black men refuse to enter, maybe it's time to stop and ask, Why? Is she looking for that *something* that cannot be gained anywhere else? What could possibly compel the estimated 70 percent Black female church community to attend church even when a questionable pastor is involved?

For African Americans, church always has been a

refuge for restoring hope. Church is where we learn to lead. Church is where we regain a sense of community. Church is where we gain lifelong friends. Church is where we remind ourselves that God is.... We go to church too because of people there who look for us every Sunday. They celebrate our joys, share in our sorrows, and care about *us*.

At church, you find out the latest news, and discover that your mother can get her blood pressure checked on Tuesday mornings at the community center. People at church notice how fast your children are growing up, and tell you about the two-for-one sale on boys' gym shoes. Dr. White, who goes to church, tells you about a simple nonprescription remedy for your ailment. Miss Johnnie Mae asks you to join the choir, where you discover that you can sing lead. Mr. Malone invites you to work with the youth, and you start coaching the basketball team that keeps twelve boys focused on something positive. God works through all of these people and experiences to let you know you are loved.

Don't let a few wanna-be preachers keep you away from the rich experiences of the community of faith. God is big enough to take care of those preachers who have perverted purposes. God's justice is not asleep; it's just more long-suffering than ours. Besides, there are many good preachers, just like there are many good brothers.

So, what are you doing this Sunday? See you in church!

FOR FURTHER MEDITATION

Prayer

Dear God, help me to heal the wounds caused by bad experiences with the church. Grant me the grace to forgive the imperfections of the church that were caused by imperfect people, for I am imperfect, too. Teach us how to live and love together as the Body of Christ. Amen.

Day 16
Breaking the Pattern

He who loves his wife loves himself.
—*Ephesians* 5:28b

"Are you ready yet?" James called.

"Almost," Adrienne answered.

Adrienne and James headed out of the apartment to attend their first premarital counseling session.

"What do you think Reverend Anderson is going to ask us?" Adrienne asked.

"I'm not sure. I've never done this before. He'll probably tell you to submit to me 'cuz I'm the head," James said, half joking.

"That's not funny, James."

"I'm sorry, but you know they always ask the bride if she will honor and obey her husband."

"James, this ain't that kind of party. If you think I'm just going to be your slave for the rest of your life, you're crazy."

"Okay, okay, be cool, baby. You know I don't think about you that way."

Adrienne and James were on their way to a full-blown argument by the time they reached the church.

"Come in, come in. How are the lovebirds today?" Reverend Anderson's greeting fell with a thud at their feet. "Are you all right?" he pressed.

"Yeah, we're all right, Reverend," replied James. "I think we're just a little nervous. Can we get started?"

"Fine," said Reverend Anderson. "Let's have a seat in my office."

They waded through the fellowship hall full of children learning how to make pottery.

After a few preliminaries, Reverend Anderson got to the meat of the matter. "Your marriage is going to be the result of a lot of influences. For over twenty years you've watched the marriages of your parents. The way they treated each other already has become a pattern, or blueprint, for you to observe. Describe your parents' marriage, James."

"Well, my father was the boss. When it came down to it, he told everybody what needed to happen. He told me and my brothers that we were all going to college . . . and we did. He told my sisters to learn to cook and clean house if they wanted to get a good husband."

"But how did your mother and father relate?" questioned Reverend Anderson.

"Well, they . . . uh . . . you know, I don't remember what kinds of things they said to each other. I do remember them arguing a lot when I was eight or nine."

Reverend Anderson probed further, asking, "What things did they argue about?"

"Well," James mumbled, "mostly Mama complained about always being tired, said there was always too much to do."

"How did you know that your parents loved each other?" Reverend Anderson continued.

"Well, Daddy always provided for her . . . for us. I don't think he was that good with saying 'I love you.'"

"James, your parents' marriage provided you with a blueprint for marriage. You have the choice of continuing the pattern or creating a new one. Do you want to repeat what you observed in your parents' marriage when you marry?"

James forced a response: "Well, I . . ."

"Don't tell me, James. Look at Adrienne and tell her," urged Reverend Anderson.

James's mind began to swim in the memories of that morning's argument. He gathered all his manly strength to restrain his swelling emotions.

"Well, James, Adrienne's waiting for you to tell her how you're going to treat her for the rest of her life."

Silently, thirty seconds of eternity passed. "It looks like you two have a lot to talk about. I'm going to leave the room and let you two discuss how you're going to relate to each other. I'll be working in the study. Just knock on the door when you're ready for me to come back in."

Just then, a crash splintered the air. A boy from the Saturday art class dropped an old clay pot. It lay shattered, with no hope of regaining its original form. "That's okay," his teacher comforted him. "Let's sweep that one up and learn how to make a new one."

FOR FURTHER MEDITATION

Prayer

Lord, male-female relationships have suffered since the fall of Adam and Eve. Reveal to me any unhealthy behavioral patterns that I may have adopted unconsciously. Teach me how to relate to all women—my spouse, my sisters, my mother, my friends—in ways that reflect godliness. Amen.

The Next Step

1. What behaviors do you remember most vividly from "the blueprint" for marriage that you observed while growing up?

2. Do you agree or disagree with any parts of that blueprint? If you are married, have you discussed them with your spouse? If not, take time to discuss each other's marriage and family blueprint.

3. After assessing your understanding of marriage, are there changes that need to occur in your own marriage and/or in your attitudes about marriage? Commit your intentions to change to the Lord and, if married, to your spouse.

Day 17
Paper Pimp

"No one can serve two masters. Either he will hate the one and love the other, or he will be devoted to the one and despise the other. You cannot serve both God and Money."
—*Matthew 6:24*

"Hey, Johnson, let me 'hold' $20."

Mr. Jenkins routinely teased every regular customer in his barbershop. Half-seriously, Johnson replied, "Man, I'll tell you what; you let me 'hold' your raggedy Buick for a week, and I'll let you 'hold' my $20."

Tim Johnson was a man with money on his mind. Johnson worked on the line at an automobile factory, making good money. But it always seemed like he wanted, needed, had to have, more money.

Coming to Jenkins's Barbershop was an adventure in "brother-life." The lazy air inside the small shop rarely moved unless coaxed by the swiveling fan on top of the soft-drink machine. Moisture from steamy towels relaxed the brute strength of salt-and-pepper beards. Each breath retrieved the mingled smells of stinging aftershave, cigarette ashes, and oily work boots. If there was no game on TV, "brother-talk" filled the void with every variety of street-corner philosophy possible. "You know, if you really want to know something.... " Some variation of these words marked the beginning of every street-corner soliloquy. Today, it was Johnson's turn.

"You know, if a brother really wants to make it these days, he's got to learn how to handle his money." A few heads looked in Johnson's direction, noticing his regular attire of green work clothes with his name embroidered on the shirt pocket. "See, I think people spend too much money on nothin'. You can't just *give* your kids everything they ask for all the time.

"Last week, Junior asked me for $150 for some 'Jordans.' I told him, 'Jordan gets his shoes for free. Why don't you get a job and buy you some regular stay-on-your-feet gym shoes.' Then my wife comes in sayin' we needs a bigger house, said she's tired of breakin' up fights between Junior and TJ. Now that they's teenagers, they needs a room to theyself. When I was growin' up, me and my two brothers slept in the same bed. I told her maybe we could fix Junior something in the basement. She wasn't satisfied; she needed a sewing room and a place for her to be, too. I don't know. . . . Houses just cost too much nowadays. A man be payin' on a house till he was half dead."

Anybody listening for the first time actually might find himself paying attention to what Johnson was saying. But when Johnson started one of his speeches, Mr. Jenkins seemed to concentrate harder on hair. He knew that something was wrong with Johnson's story. One day he started adding things up. *Let's see*, thought Mr. Jenkins, *Johnson makes good money and works a lot of overtime, too. I never see him dressed in anything but those work clothes during the daytime. He's been driving that same old too-long-for-him Cadillac for years now. His wife and kids are always complaining because he won't get up off of any money. Where is all that long green going?* Something was wrong.

Mr. Jenkins didn't feel it was his place to get into

Johnson's business, so he never asked him what he actually did with his money. One thing became clear, though: Johnson was driven by money. Every time he talked, the subject of money came up. *Maybe he just likes saving it; or maybe he's got somebody on the side,* thought Mr. Jenkins.

Any way you looked at it, as much as Johnson thought he was in control, the truth of the matter is that money was controlling him. Money told him when to get up, what to do, and how long to do it. He didn't realize that nobody really paid him any mind, because he didn't care about anything but his money.

I bet if he lost his job he'd go crazy, thought Mr. Jenkins. *It's sad. Johnson could be a decent brother. But right now, he ain't nothin' but a paper pimp who gets used in the process.*

FOR FURTHER MEDITATION

Prayer

Lord, show me the other gods in my life. Release me from my attachment to money and materialism. Break its stranglehold on my life. Amen.

Day 18
Absent Presence

God can testify how I long for all of you with the affection of Christ Jesus.

—Philippians 1:8

 y daddy lives in California. He said he's gonna send me a plane ticket and take me to Disneyland one day. He sends me stuff in the mail all the time, man, all the time...."

Rudy defended his father's absence as best a nine-year-old can. His parents divorced when he was almost three. It wasn't unusual; half of his friends had absent fathers.

When Rudy got together with his friends, they swapped stories about whose daddy was "the baddest." Most of the conversations centered around what gifts they got from their fathers. Little was mentioned about needing to spend time with their fathers. Maybe young boys don't realize how much they need to see their fathers until a little later in life.

It had been four years since Rudy's father, DeAngelo, had moved from Chicago to somewhere in California. Rudy never could remember what city his father lived in. He only knew about Los Angeles, San Diego, Oakland, and San Francisco because they had pro teams there. His daddy lived in one of those "other cities." In those four years, Rudy's imagination had stayed up nights creating and re-creating possible images of his father. He vaguely remembered the time when DeAngelo tossed him in the air as Rudy's mother screamed, "If you drop that boy, I'll divorce you!" Aside from that, his memory could do no better than recall a tall, strong, ebony-colored hulk of a man with a room-filling laugh. It didn't matter much to Rudy why his father and mother had broken up. He just knew he was supposed to see his father sometimes.

DeAngelo tried to do right by his son. He sent the monthly support money on time. He called Rudy at least two or three times a month, and even dropped him something special in the mail from time to time. He wanted to spend more time with Rudy, but California was too far away for a nine-year-old to travel to alone. DeAngelo couldn't afford the regular plane fares; he was barely making it after starting over. He was in the construction business, so he had to work when there was work. And when he wasn't working, he knew that the next job might be only a phone call away.

DeAngelo really missed Rudy during basketball season. DeAngelo had been a star high school player. When Rudy was born, DeAngelo dreamed about teaching Rudy how to play the game he loved so dearly.

Somehow, Rudy's got to know that I'll always be there for him even though we're so far apart, DeAngelo thought. He loved his son. That night, he wrestled with sleep. *God, how am I going to make a difference in my son's life?* he thought, half to heaven and half to himself.

The next morning, a persistent idea hung in his thoughts: *Why don't you go visit Rudy?* DeAngelo toyed with the idea over his morning coffee. *I've been working steady with my foreman for two years. I haven't missed a day of work. It's about time for me to get a break. I'll explain everything and ask for Thursday, Friday, and Monday off. I can drive to L.A., and take one of those cheap flights to*

Chicago. I remember them advertising those special one-way fares this month. I can stay with my cousin Freddie, and maybe we can take Rudy to a Bulls game. In just a few minutes, DeAngelo had worked out the details.

As the plane rose into the morning haze that Thursday, DeAngelo closed his eyes and thought of how God had made a way for him to visit Rudy. It seemed like God was just waiting for DeAngelo to make up his mind to make a difference in Rudy's life. He discovered that he could still be present with Rudy, even from a long distance.

FOR FURTHER MEDITATION

Prayer

For Fathers

Dear Lord, my children need my love, even from a distance. Show me how to love them so that they always will know that I care and support them. Amen.

For Other Men

Dear Lord, I may not have children of my own, but I see so many children whose fathers are not present in their lives. Help me to make a difference in at least one young life by taking time to be the father-figure he or she needs. Amen.

Day 19

It's You, Brother... you!

O LORD, you have searched me and you know me.
—Psalm 139:1

It's you she loves, brother... you! That's sometimes hard to believe. Maybe it's because of all the "stuff" that makes up the American dream: nice cars, big house, good job, and much money. These are the supposed signs of success. God has a way of challenging that dream within the marriage context. Do you struggle to understand that your wife really loves *you*—not the stuff? Or, if you're not married, do you struggle to understand that you don't need the stuff to get a woman to love you?

Maybe our upbringing muddies the issue for us. Many of us are raised to believe that a "real man" finds work, and provides for his wife and family. Furthermore, any brother worth his salt will "protect" his wife and family by any means necessary. The work ethic and the macho image are promoted as the epitome of successful manhood. Notice, however, what is conspicuously absent from our training: relationship-building.

In general, women experience a different kind of socialization. They are groomed to prepare for the marriage relationship. Learning how to interact with the male ego and the male psyche are common points of discussion. Discovering how to develop the relationship is the focal point for them. When men and women come together after such vastly different upbringings, misunderstanding is a predictable result.

You then enter the tug-of-war of the ages. You love her and want to marry her. But you also want her to know from the beginning that you are not a worthless, "get-over," sit-up-in-the-house-all-day-no-workin' brother. Your cloudy thinking fails to inform you that she already knew you were a good man, or else she wouldn't have agreed to marry you in the first place. She loves *you*, brother... YOU!

If you consider the words of the psalmist, you realize that God knows you intimately as well. God knows your thoughts, your motives, and your whereabouts. God takes special interest in you. You are fearfully and wonderfully made, with a divine destiny before you. The next time you're in front of the mirror, look beyond that receding hairline, sliding chest, and ballooning belly to discover the you that God sees. Remember: God loves *you*, brother... YOU!

FOR FURTHER MEDITATION

Prayer

Dear Lord, help me to see that my real self-worth comes from things that money cannot provide. Show me those godly qualities that really define manhood and personal value. Amen.

The Next Step

1. How much of your self-image is tied up with your ability to get and hold a job?

2. List the qualities apart from your job that make you a man.

3. Develop the habit of regularly thanking God for these qualities.

Day 20
You'll Never Be the Same

*I want men everywhere to lift up holy hands in prayer,
without anger or disputing.*

—1 Timothy 2:8

To pray is to change. Leroy didn't realize that at first.
The only types of prayers he'd heard while growing up
were "Lord, have mercy" prayers, "Lord, help me"
prayers, and "Fix it, Lord" prayers. Nobody ever talked
about what happens to you when you pray.

Well into his adult life, Leroy's prayers were no
different. Every Thanksgiving, he felt like his draft
number came up when he had to say a special blessing
over the food—with all the relatives watching.
Spontaneous, from-the-heart praying was different;
people expected you to say something you felt. This
wasn't easy for Leroy. He was used to repeating the
regular blessing his daddy always prayed: "We thank
the Lord for the nourishment we're about to receive,
for Christ's sake. A-men." Leroy could say it in his
sleep in a sing-song rhythm that made his children bob
their heads mockingly.

Whenever someone called on Leroy to pray, it was
always the same—except on Thanksgiving, or Christmas.
Then, Leroy got dramatic and prayed that same prayer
slowly, with a long pause after *Lord* and before *Amen*.

Every year his relatives held their breath and tried to keep their groans from slipping out. After "prayin'," Leroy would smile, pat his stomach, and quote his grandfather's favorite scripture: "Arise, Peter; slay and eat" (Acts 11:7 KJV).

One day Leroy came home from work disgusted. Jones, his supervisor, had been riding him about increasing production and cutting down on defective parts. *What's wrong with him?* Leroy thought. *He knows I can't do anything about those defects. I get the parts from the press department. If they let something slide, I wind up with a bad part. He should be talking to them.*

Leroy felt harassed for weeks. Finally his wife, Carol, encouraged him to pray about it. Leroy grunted an "okay" and went for a drive to get some ice cream. Somehow a bowl of vanilla ice cream and four or five chocolate chip cookies made him think better.

He came back and started "think-praying" with God. *Lord, you know what I've been going through at work. It doesn't make any sense. God, you've got to do something with Jones before he drives all of us crazy.* This "think-praying" went on for weeks without Leroy noticing anything.

Three weeks later, Carol asked him what happened at work.

"What do you mean, what happened at work? Nothing! I still go, and we still make the same old parts. Jimmy's on vacation, so I have to help his replacement learn the ropes. Besides that, it's the same ol' same ol'."

Leroy was puzzled by her question. Carol always seemed to sense things that Leroy didn't even notice.

Carol explained her question: "Well, I've just been noticing that you aren't complaining about Jones lately. Did he move to another department or something?"

"No, he's still around," Leroy replied. "But now that you mention it, he just hasn't been getting on my nerves lately. It's kind of funny. Waymon, Floyd, and I just decided that Jones was getting old and needed a vacation. After a while, I hardly noticed him poking around with his pencil and clipboard. Yesterday it was pretty hot in the plant, and I even bought old Jones a can of pop."

Carol's eyes twinkled. "Looks to me like your praying paid off, huh?"

"Yeah," Leroy admitted, almost embarrassed. "Here I was praying for God to fix Jones, and I wound up changing. It just seemed like I started understanding Jones better, and it didn't seem worth it to be mad at him all the time. Now that I think about it, I remember feeling kind of sorry for him because he doesn't have a lot a friends. Maybe when he saw me lighten up, he lightened up, too."

Leroy chuckled and started shaking his head. *God sure taught me something about prayer today,* he thought. *I guess I better not ever pray unless I'm ready to change.*

FOR FURTHER MEDITATION

Prayer

Dear Lord, today I offer myself to you in prayer. I welcome you to mold and shape me in the process. Amen.

Spiritual Exercise

God's answers to prayer sometimes involve changes in others, changes in circumstances, or changes in us. The next time you pray, be open to God making changes in any of these areas.

Day 21
All Over Again

And the God of all grace, who called you to his eternal glory in Christ, after you have suffered a little while, will himself restore you and make you strong, firm and steadfast.
—1 Peter 5:10

Don't *want* nobody else . . . don't *need* nobody else. Marie, there's nobody like you."

Jerome gently laid flowers on the one-year-old grave of his deceased wife. This year had seemed to grow extra days, longer hours, and darker midnights. He didn't talk to his family much anymore. Grief and mourning had lured him into a hermit-like existence.

The memories of Marie were bittersweet for Jerome. As he remembered scattered events from their thirty-two years of marriage, a smile stretched across his face. She always made things better. No power? "Let's eat by candlelight," she would say. No paycheck for a while? "Baby, I can do more with gravy and cornbread than most folks can do with meat and potatoes," she would tell him.

Even the memory of their fights brought a chuckle to Jerome's lips; like the time he was on that money-saving kick. Every spare dollar went into the bank unless some real emergency came up. Funny how men's emergencies are different from women's emergencies. When Marie came home one day with a new dress for Baby-girl to wear

74

to the prom, Jerome thought she had lost her natural-born mind.

"It was an emergency," Marie pleaded in defense.

"How?" Jerome asked.

"Baby-girl needs a decent dress to go out in, and Mardelle's was having a 75-percent-off sale. That's an emergency!" Marie said defiantly.

They argued for three hours straight, with one "rest stop" in the middle—when Jerome had to go to the bathroom. Arguing just stirs stuff up in a man sometimes. Marie then played her trump card. She walked to Baby-girl's closet and pulled out what used to be Baby-girl's best dress.

"You want her to wear this to the prom?" she questioned.

"Yeah! What's wrong with that?" Jerome knew he had her then; Baby-girl had worn that dress only once, and that was to Aunt Tootie's wedding out of state. Marie made him look closer.

"Look!" she said. And then he saw.

"Smell that . . . feel this . . . now pull on that hem just a little."

He did, and the fool thing almost fell apart in his hands—dry rot.

"You want Baby-girl to wear this?" Marie asked again. "One good dance move, and that dress would split from here to heaven, showing ever'thing that should be a secret to them hungry little boys."

He just started laughing. "Marie, you should'a been a lawyer. You tried that case like Perry Mason."

Memories. They were all precious to him now.

Before Jerome left the graveyard, he prayed a silent prayer: *Lord, I sure do miss Marie, but I know you're taking better care of her now than I ever could. Tell her I love her still.* Just then, Jerome started to feel warm all over, like God was talking back to him, smiling. It was as if Jerome finally had let Marie go and God was telling him it was all right to go on with his life.

Jerome slipped on his old crumpled-up hat and walked back to his car, relieved. *Maybe I'll go visit some of my grandchildren after school today. I don't think I ever told them about how I almost played pro ball, till my left knee started paining me.*

FOR FURTHER MEDITATION

Prayer

Dear Lord, walk with me through my grief. You are the author of new beginnings. Show me how to live my life from this point forward. Inspire me to be a blessing to others. Amen.

Run, Joseph! Run!

Now Joseph was well-built and handsome, and after a while his master's wife took notice of Joseph and said, "Come to bed with me!"

—Genesis 39:6b-7

m! Um! Um! Marcus, did you see that? That sistuh's got everything a man needs to die happy!"

Marcus's friend and colleague Antonio loved to drool over women. Just then *she* walked by. Marcus had to admit, Antonio was not exaggerating.

"Who is she?" Marcus tried to ask nonchalantly.

Marcus was married with three children. Antonio called him one of those "sho-nuff married brothers."

"I think her name is Kim," Antonio said with a smirk. "She's from California, you know. Just look at that sun-kissed brown skin; long, black, down-your-back hair; and California curves all over the place. Somebody needs to check out her—"

"Antonio!" Marcus interrupted in disgust. "Man, I just asked you for her name not the six o'clock news!"

Antonio backed off. "Look, Marc, I'm just saying, you don't see fine women like Kim every day."

Several weeks passed without incident. Then it happened. Nancy, Marcus's secretary, took maternity leave and personnel transferred Kim to Marcus's department.

"Hi, I'm Nancy's temporary replacement," Kim announced with a smile.

Marcus never imagined anything would happen. His wedding band was on constant display, and he wasn't looking for anyone else. Besides, having Kim as his private secretary would drive Antonio crazy.

Kim and Marcus worked well together. She was efficient and accurate, and she even made some suggestions that noticeably improved his quarterly reports. Kim was so thoughtful. She had coffee ready in the mornings, didn't mind working late, and she smelled like fresh roses. While her voice was always professional, it seemed to have an alluring quality. Her dresses were tasteful but fit quite well in all the right places. After a while, Marcus caught himself wishing that Kim would be his permanent secretary. He could give Kim things to do that he wouldn't dream of asking Nancy to do.

Marcus considered himself a pretty progressive boss who knew how to keep his coworkers happy and motivated. So when Professional Secretaries Day came, he ordered a modest mug of flowers for Kim, and offered to take her to lunch. Kim suggested they finish the Riley report first and then take a late lunch. Marcus agreed. They went to Ming's Garden for Chinese, and enjoyed good food and pleasant conversation. They left and walked to Marcus's jet black BMW. He turned the key; nothing happened. He accidentally had left his lights on. Kim quickly invited him to her nearby apartment where he could call the motor club. Marcus pushed past his initial hesitancy and finally said okay.

Kim's apartment was impressive. Strips of mudcloth from Mali smartly accented her coffee tables. Limited-edition Charles Bibbs prints hung, begging for attention.

"Oh, shoot. I've got a run in my panty hose," Kim blurted. "The phone's over there; help yourself. I'll be right back."

Before Marcus could protest, Kim disappeared behind her bedroom door. Quickly, Marcus dialed the motor club; they said they would be there in forty minutes.

Kim emerged from her bedroom wearing some white shorts and a matching half-blouse that complemented her "California brown skin."

"Whew, that's better," she said. "I get tired of being professional all day, don't you?" She eased herself next to Marcus, and began showing him her photo album. "See, I was Miss Bakersfield when I was in college. That's the one-piece bathing suit they wouldn't let me wear in the finals. They said it needed more material before they would consider it a bathing suit. Ooh, it's hot in here. Let me get you something cool to drink."

Kim left the photo album open to the "Bakersfield" page and went to pour some iced tea.

By now Marcus was feeling very uneasy. Little beads of sweat formed on his receding hairline. He tried to swallow the lump in his throat as he mentally fought off the sneaky seduction he felt pulling him. *This is not cool,* he thought.

Kim returned with the tea. "What's wrong, Marcus? You look a little tense. Why don't you let me rub your temples? People say I make them relax. I thought about being a masseuse once."

Marcus stood up quickly. "That's okay. You know, I think the motor club likes for you to stay by your vehicle so they don't have to wait. I think I'd better go now. Thanks for letting me use the phone."

Marcus hurried out of the apartment. As he rode down the elevator he realized just how close he had come to ruining seven years of marriage.

FOR FURTHER MEDITATION

Prayer

Dear Lord, remind me that seduction's grip is deadly. Give me the good sense to flee from sexual and sensual temptations immediately. Amen.

Day 23

"Married, with Children"

Let us not become weary in doing good, for at the proper time we will reap a harvest if we do not give up.

—*Galatians 6:9*

Neither Audrey nor Melvin could believe it. They had been going out for only six months; now they were married. After suffering through a terrible first marriage, Audrey had vowed never to marry again. Melvin, likewise, had endured enough bad relationships to retire romance from his vocabulary. Ah, but love changes things, doesn't it? One day you're single, and the next day you wake up to words like... "Melvin, can you take us to the store?"

A pair of persistent little hands pulled on Melvin's unfortunate arm. This marriage came with a ready-made family. Audrey had two children: six-year-old Terrel, and his two-year-old sister, Geraldine. Melvin struggled to let go of "those last five minutes of sleep." He rolled over and tried to shield his eyes from the rays of morning sunlight.

"Terrel, what's happening, buddy?" Melvin asked. "Let's wait till the stores open—in about three hours."

Melvin wasn't quite ready to share his early-morning time and space with Terrel and Geraldine. He imagined that children somehow could be quarantined in their rooms until the "normal" waking hours of the day. This idea of "sharing" his new wife with her children—their children—was a struggle.

Melvin was beginning to learn what becoming an instant daddy is all about. At first, Terrel was a cute, energetic little boy with an adorable, rambunctious little shadow named Geraldine. One month into married life, Melvin began to reassess his original impressions. *Don't these kids ever sleep at the same time?* he wondered. *Why do they have to scream like their hair's on fire? Do all children eat eight times a day? Why do they have to have so many new school clothes? Is this what it's going to be like until they go to college? Something's got to change around here.*

The hardest times for Melvin were when Audrey's "ex" came to visit the children. If he remembered to send child support, it was always late. But when he showed up, he was Mr. Sugar Daddy, full of expensive gifts. He brought Terrel that addictive videogame. He spoiled the kids with designer jeans and expensive gym shoes. After these visits, Melvin felt like a bomb had exploded; he became the bad guy when he wouldn't continue to supply the kids with the same kind of expensive gifts. Sometimes it was more than he could handle. Fortunately, he had a friend, Walter, who was "married, with children."

Melvin got in the car and wound up at Walter's house. Walter had married into a ready-made family, too. He and Wanda had just celebrated eight years together.

Melvin needed some advice.

"Walter, how did you make it with Wanda and her kids when you first got married?" Melvin asked.

Walter smiled and just shook his head. "Man, it wasn't easy at first," he said. "I didn't feel like I was the daddy in the house until four years into it. I think the only thing that kept my sanity was reading magazine articles and books about blended families. I found out that it takes one to three years for couples to become married if there are no children involved. If there are children, it takes four to six years to become married *and* family.

"You're learning two roles at the same time, brother. Give yourself some time to adjust. Remember a couple of things: Audrey is always going to have a special relationship with her kids. They have a history together, and you've got to let them have that special bond. Those kids also have a relationship with their father. He has a right to visit them, and they always may have some loyalties with him that they won't have with you. That's part of the territory.

"Those kids will have to make a decision one day about whom they are going to trust as their father. You just keep loving them, and don't get tired of doing what's right. They're going to make their choice one way or the other. Just remember, you married Audrey so that the two of you could live the rest of your lives together. The children have to decide what role they want to play in this new family. Look, there's no guarantee that if you had your own blood children that they would totally respect you. God was Adam and Eve's parent, and they chose to listen to another voice. Don't stop doing what's right, or you'll look back on these years and be sorry."

"Thanks, Walter," Melvin said as he shook hands with his good friend. On the way home, he thought more about what Walter had said. *Well,* Melvin thought, *I'm going to do my part, and whatever happens, happens.*

At home, Terrel ran up to the car door, grinning and shouting: "Can we go? Can we go?"

"Go where?" Melvin asked.

"To the father-and-son banquet at school. You my daddy, ain't you?"

FOR FURTHER MEDITATION

Prayer

For All Fathers

Dear Lord, teach me the blessing of showing fatherly love to my children. Lord, be my encouragement when parenting gets discouraging. Amen.

For Other Men

Dear Lord, I know I don't have to be a father to show fatherly love. There are children all around me who need encouragement, hope, and love. Help me to be a positive influence in the lives of all the children I meet each day. Amen.

Day 24

Grandfathers and Good Sense

Encourage the young men to be self-controlled. In everything set them an example by doing what is good. In your teaching show integrity, seriousness and soundness of speech that cannot be condemned, so that those who oppose you may be ashamed because they have nothing bad to say about us.

—Titus 2:6-8

How do grandfathers come by their good sense? Is it because they've lived so much longer than the next generation? Were people just tougher in "those days"? Or, are grandfathers a special gift that God gives to every generation?

Dorian's grandfather seemed to know everything about baseball. Gramps's love for the game was contagious, and Dorian was incurably infected. Dorian loved to spend the night with his grandparents. He and Gramps would pop popcorn and stay up until "the wee hours of the morning" listening to baseball games on the radio. Gramps's old brown RCA radio wasn't partial. It picked up Cubs day games, White Sox night games, and Braves home and road games. On good nights, it even tuned in the St. Louis Cardinals. Gramps took Dorian to every Braves game he could in his lime green '56 Buick. On the way, he sometimes let Dorian blow the horn. Ahhhhh Oooooooh Gahhhhhhh. Parking was twenty-five cents, bleacher seats were fifty cents, and children under twelve got in free. Dorian and his grandfather saw some of the great ones play: Hank Aaron, Willie Mays, Dick Allen, Maury Wills, Lou Brock, Don Drysdale, and Sandy Koufax. Gramps taught Dorian how to appreciate real talent.

In between showing Dorian how to figure out batting averages, Gramps taught Dorian about life and self-control. "What's wrong, you stupid ump? He was safe by a mile!" Dorian shouted during one game.

Gramps quickly corrected the rough edges of youth. "Watch your language, Dorian!" His words had power because Gramps never cussed. Gramps taught Dorian to be a student of the game and a student of life. Dorian learned a thousand subtle lessons each time he talked with his grandfather. Gramps was the only grandfather Dorian knew. That's why after Gramps died Dorian missed him so. There would never be another Gramps. But sometimes God gives us other grandfathers.

When Dorian was fourteen, Mr. Hunter became prominent in Dorian's life. Mr. Hunter seemed to be made of the same stock as Gramps. He taught Dorian about music—and life. Saturday mornings became an adventure in discovery. While waiting for his organ lesson, Dorian thumbed through the science magazines lying around. Mr. Hunter was a proficient electronics engineer, piano repairman, model train enthusiast, and minister of music. After a few years, their relationship blossomed. Seeing Dorian's keen interest in music, Mr. Hunter often invited Dorian to accompany him. They drove to Chicago for piano parts in Mr. Hunter's long, gold Eldorado.

"Dorian, why don't you drive?" Mr. Hunter suggested. "I've never ridden in the passenger seat." Mr. Hunter instilled such confidence in Dorian.

In church, Mr. Hunter encouraged Dorian to prepare songs to play during the offering. After weeks of motivating and praising Dorian's efforts, he arranged for the church to hear more of Dorian's playing and less of his own. Before he knew it, Dorian was playing during the entire church service. How do grandfathers get to be so smart?

Over the years, Dorian realized that God had placed many grandfathers in his life. His Little League coach, Mr. David, taught him more about the fundamentals of baseball and life. "If you don't see me do it, don't do it. If you don't hear me say it, don't say it," he would say. Mr. David led by example. Tony King taught Dorian how to "think" musically, and how to appreciate the genius of African American art forms. Reverend Goodlette pushed him to be a leader and take on new responsibilities. Reverend "Pop" McCutcheon taught him to be patient with people, persistent in work, and Christian in attitude.

These men were Dorian's standard-bearers—seasoned and settled. They had survived the Depression, world wars, segregation, and untold prejudice. But hardship hadn't hardened them. Somehow they each had come to terms with life, and had chosen to live above the odds against them. Their mellowed maturity quietly commanded respect. Their crucial influence molded maturing minds. Without them, Dorian would be less than a man. Without them, Dorian would be a walking exterior, waiting to be filled with substance. If Dorian rose to great heights, it was because he stood on the shoulders of grandfathers and good sense.

FOR FURTHER MEDITATION

Prayer

Dear Lord, thank you for the blessing of older men in my life. Prepare me to be a similar blessing someday. Amen.

Day 25

On My One Good Leg!

Though now for a little while you may have had to suffer grief in all kinds of trials. These have come so that your faith—of greater worth than gold, which perishes even though refined by fire—may be proved genuine and may result in praise, glory and honor when Jesus Christ is revealed.

—1 Peter 1:6-7

Go, Randy! Go, Randy! Go, Randy! Go, Randy!

"Look at him," Wilbur said to his date as they left the dance floor. "Randy sure enjoys life, doesn't he?"

Wilbur pulled Randy aside. "Hey, man, take a rest for a minute. You're making me tired. Where do you get all that energy?"

"Well," said Randy, smiling, "after what I've been through, I decided to be glad that I'm even alive. I wasn't always like this, though...." Randy remembered how desperate he had felt just a few years ago.

"My unit was one of the first to be called overseas to fight for our country," Randy continued. "That tour of duty seemed like one endless night of terror. They never tell you about everything that happens in war. I guess if they did, nobody but crazy folks would go. One Friday evening changed my life forever.

"I had night duty. Everything seemed peaceful enough

until I heard the sound of missiles cutting through the air. 'Hit it!' I screamed, and all of my troop scrambled for cover. I climbed down from my perch and started running for the nearest bunker. That's when the flash of light came. One of the bombs exploded just yards away from me. That's all I remembered until I woke up in a medical helicopter.

"I heard a lot of guys screaming, 'They shot us; our own guys shot us!' We were victims of what they call 'friendly fire.' Forty percent of my body was burned, and my left leg was full of shrapnel.

"I remember seeing the doctors in the operating room shake their heads as one of them said, 'We'll have to take it.' They amputated my left leg just above the knee. I spent weeks in the burn unit recovering from my first skin graft. While I was there, I had a lot of time to think. There were many days I didn't even want to live. I remember praying, 'God, why didn't you just take me? Now I've got to live the rest of my life like some freak of war.' God didn't seem to answer me.

"Then I started thinking about who I was and who I wanted to be. Somewhere in the back of my mind, I always knew I was good with my hands. You know, building and fixing things came easy to me. I figured I could learn about electronics or something, if I just put my mind to it.

"Before long, I had a full-fledged dream going. I got excited and started reading up on the kind of training available. I didn't realize it at the time, but God was answering my cry for help. The Lord gave me a new hope to build on.

"I didn't need two legs to work in electronics. In the process, I realized that no bomb could stop me from being an electrician, a husband, a father, or a man. When I stop to think about it, I guess the Lord was showing me that nothing short of himself can stop me from being what he wants me to be.

"I knew I was all right one day when two of my friends came by to see me. They walked in, trying to feel sorry for me and looking all sad in the mouth. I couldn't take it. I got mad. I looked them square in the eye and said, 'Listen, you can keep your old pity party. I can do more on my one good leg than both of you put together.' That's when I knew God had given me the will to live again. So that's my story, Wilbur.

"I'd like to keep talking, but I promised Martha one more dance. Uh oh, that's my song. I'll see you later."

Randy resumed his place on the dance floor—a picture of ebony grace, swaying and bobbing on his one good leg.

FOR FURTHER MEDITATION

Prayer

Dear Lord, forgive me for having pity parties when I should be thankful for just being alive. Help me to realize that as long as you allow me to live, I have a purpose to fulfill in this lifetime. Thank you for giving me another day of life. Amen.

Day 26

Give Me Some SPACE!

Very early in the morning, while it was still dark, Jesus got up, left the house and went off to a solitary place, where he prayed.

—**Mark 1:35**

t *the office:*

Coworker: C'mon, Charlie! Why don't you sit with us for lunch sometime?

Charles: My name is Charles, not Charlie!

Coworker: Whatever. Anyhow, there's a seat here. Why don't you eat with us today?

Charles (thinking to himself): Why is it that every time there's a racism or diversity seminar, my white coworkers begin to move with "all deliberate" speed to be inclusive? Yesterday, I wasn't even the last thought on their minds. Inclusive? Oh yeah. That's a code word for "please assimilate your cultural values, tone down your way of speaking, and entertain my newfound desire to 'learn' about people of color." I don't have time to be "on" during my lunch—to appease somebody else's guilty conscience. I refuse to be the latest novelty.

Later, at home:

Linda: Sweetheart, what's wrong? You don't seem to be yourself today. Did something happen at work?
Charles: No, baby. I'm just a little tired; that's all.
Linda: Charles, talk to me. I want to listen. When you hurt, I hurt. I want to know, sweetheart.
Charles: It's nothing . . . really.

God really made us different. Why do wives have such a great hunger for intimate, transparent relationships? We men don't like to admit it, but most of us haven't learned how to express ourselves intimately.

Then enters six-year-old Wyndell:

Wyndell: Daddy, Daddy, Jimmie let me play with his computer odyssey game. I almost made it to level six, where you can turn invisible when Maniac Mike comes at you. Can we get one? You said I'm getting bigger now. I'm in the first grade, and Miss Smith says computers stim-a-late your mind. Can we get one, Daddy, PLEEEEEEEEEASE?
Charles: We'll see, Wyndell. We'll see.

In the Bible, Old Testament believers created sacred spaces for themselves and God. Men erected altars of stone or wood to designate a meeting place with God—apart from the pull of people. If there was no physical altar, Jewish men would pull their prayer shawls over their heads and make a tent or tabernacle. This created a sacred "tent of meeting" for themselves and God. We need sacred places carved out of our otherwise normal space. These "alone places" are prayer places, regroup-ing-and-rediscovering-purpose spaces. Here, we regain perspective, purge our prerogatives, and examine our motives. We need confessing places, inspirational places, and spiritual communion spaces. We need keeping-our-sanity and calming-our-nerves places. We crave remembering places and daring-to-be-different spaces. We blossom again in recreative places and learning-to-live spaces. We mend relationships in forgiving places. We rebound in dust-yourself-off-and-move-on spaces. We're reborn in inspirational places. We could use a good dose of recalling-where-you've-come-from-to-determine-where-you're-headed spaces.

> Very early in the morning, while it was still dark, Jesus got up, left the house and went off to a solitary place, where he prayed. (Mark 1:35)

Hmm, if Jesus needed some space . . . .

FOR FURTHER MEDITATION

Prayer

Dear Lord, the pull of other people on my life sometimes overwhelms me. Draw me away to a solitary place to be alone with you and myself. Amen.

Day 27

Love Is All Around Us

Love is patient, love is kind. It does not envy, it does not boast, it is not proud. It is not rude, it is not self-seeking, it is not easily angered, it keeps no record of wrongs. Love does not delight in evil but rejoices with the truth. It always protects, always trusts, always hopes, always perseveres. Love never fails.

*—1 Corinthians 13:4-8*a

ove is a force."
Amen!

"Martin Luther King, Jr. believed in the power of agape, God's unconditional, uncompromising love."
Yessuh!

"Love draws a man and a woman together, no matter what the distance or the obstacle."
Say it!

"Love pursues injustice and demands recompense."
Preach on!

"Love stands while others cower."
Well!

"Love promotes peace without a pistol."
Uh huh!

"Love wrapped itself in human flesh, came down, and dwelt among us...."

Victor listened to fragments of Reverend Bertram's

sermon before drifting into his own thoughts. *How does this love thing play out in real life?* he wondered. *Martin's dream got him killed. Men and women come together, but a lot of them don't stay together. Jesus was there for the disciples, but I can't see him. If love is so strong, it ought to make the six o'clock news.* Victor was in a blue funk because he was experiencing the American nightmare—no job, no car, no home, and no woman.

Independent thoughts began to invade his silent fuss. Flashes of faces streamed across his memory. *What's Grandma, Uncle Mike, Michelle, and DeMarcus got to do with this?* Victor seemed to be an involuntary spectator of the scene. One by one, each character enticed him to revisit some vivid experience from the past.

Grandma always had time for him. One time she stopped snapping beans and walked him back to Mr. John Day's store because Victor said Mr. Day had cheated him. He remembers how proud he was of his grandmother for standing up for him. Grandma trusted Victor and treated him with such kindness.

Uncle Mike took him by the hand and put some shoulder pads on him. "Stay low, Victor," he told him. "Now drive your shoulder into his legs. Yeah, that's how to throw a cross-block."

Uncle Mike drilled Victor every weekend that summer. Victor was trying out for the high school football team.

"You can make varsity if you want it bad enough. Get up and try it again, Victor; you've got to have some heart, brother."

Victor learned an unforgettable lesson in perseverance. He still remembers how proud he was to show Uncle Mike his varsity letter after the season.

Michelle walked by, and Victor's memories followed her to South L.A. They walked past a wanna-be gangsta' running his mouth at everything that moved.

"How can you live here and listen to all that mess these brothers say?" questioned Victor.

"Look, Victor, I know who I am; they're still wondering who they are. If they keep living, they'll wake up. I just can't let somebody else's negativity get me down."

Victor wished he could stay cool under pressure like Michelle.

They bumped into DeMarcus at the community center. He was teaching an art class from his wheelchair. Four months ago he caught a stray bullet from a drive-by shooting just outside this same center. Victor remembered his confusion at the time.

"DeMarcus, some of these brothers belong to the gang. They're the ones that shot you. How can you turn around and teach them about art?" DeMarcus just smiled and said, "Victor, if we keep turning our backs on *us*, where will *we* be?"

Reverend Bertram's sermon rose to a crescendo, snapping Victor back to reality. "Love is like an unstoppable army. Let's call the roll from love's ranks. Patience! Kindness! Hope! Perseverance! Trust! All present and accounted for, sir. Listen, there can be no arrogance or evil here. No, sir! There can be no grudges or selfishness here. No, sir! So you see, my brothers and my sisters, love is a mighty force."

Amen!

"Don't be surprised if God hasn't already begun sending recruiters to your house. If we're honest, none of us has escaped the long arm of God's love. Look closely. Love is all around us."

Amen, preacha'!

FOR FURTHER MEDITATION

Prayer

Lord, open my eyes to recognize demonstrations of

your love in everyday situations. Thank you for bringing loving people into my life. Show me how to love in practical, meaningful ways. Amen.

Spiritual Exercise

God often speaks to us through our experiences with people. Take time to reflect on the times when people have been loving toward you. These are the moments when God also is speaking to you.

Day 28

When Heaven Shuts Its Mouth

Husbands, in the same way be considerate as you live with your wives, and treat them with respect as the weaker partner and as heirs with you of the gracious gift of life, so that nothing will hinder your prayers.

—*1 Peter 3:7*

C'mon, y'all. We're gonna be late." Brother Hezekiah Moore wouldn't tolerate anyone making him late for church. He was the chairman of the deacon board, and in charge of the adult Sunday school class. "Mabel, what's takin' y'all so long? Hurry up!" he called.

Brother Moore's wife had her hands full trying to gather their three squirming little children every Sunday morning. Five-year-old Bobby always had a runny nose. The three-year-old twins, Sharice and Shantell, seemed to take turns spilling things on themselves whenever Mabel went to get dressed. Sunday was no day of rest for Mabel. Her job was to wake the children, feed everybody, and press everyone's Sunday clothes before getting herself ready for church. Meanwhile, Brother Moore sipped his morning coffee, read the paper, and reviewed the Sunday school lesson. Then, when he got to church, he could "break open the Word" for folks who didn't know.

Somehow, Mabel miraculously pushed everyone out of the house in the next five minutes, and they were on their way. Brother Moore pulled into the church parking lot and carefully backed his Lincoln town car into the shade under the sugar maple tree. They all piled out of the car: Sharice and Shantell, with their frilly white dresses and lace-edged socks; Bobby, with his blue three-piece suit that he would grow into by the end of the year; and Mabel, with her white pleated skirt with the matching short jacket, and her white wide-brim hat with black edging. Since it was "first Sunday," Brother Moore wore his black suit, crisp white shirt, and black bow tie. He carried his white Communion gloves in a baggy in his inside jacket pocket.

Brother Moore went straight to class. As usual, Stanley was the first one there. People said Stanley was a little slow in the mind, but he was a sincere and faithful member. After the opening prayer, Brother Moore began reviewing the highlights of the day's lesson. He read 1 Peter 3:7, and began to "break open the Word."

"See," he explained, "this scripture is saying that men need to respect their wives and be considerate. If you don't, it could hinder your prayers."

Stanley raised his hand. "Brother Moore," he asked, "does God talk to you?"

Brother Moore sighed and said, "Yes, Stanley, of course God talks to me. I'm a Christian."

Stanley continued, "Well, what does he say to you? Did he talk to you this morning?"

Brother Moore started losing his patience. "No, God didn't say anything in particular to me this morning. God speaks when he's ready."

Stanley seemed compelled to press the point. "Maybe God's mad with you, if you didn't hear from him this morning. Sometimes my daddy just shuts up when he's sick of me."

Brother Moore looked at his watch as he said, "Well,

our time is getting away from us. Let's move on to the rest of the lesson."

After class, Brother Moore quickly went up to the sanctuary for worship. This was Communion Sunday, and Reverend Samuels did something different. He spent a long time talking about reconciling with people and with God.

"Scripture tells us to 'get right' with people before we give our offering," he said. "Scripture tells us to settle quickly with our adversaries. And Scripture tells us to examine ourselves before we take Communion. Take a few moments of silence to examine your week with God. Carry on a dialogue with the Master."

Brother Moore dutifully bowed his head. Unconsciously, he started mouthing some of his routine prayers to God. Then a strange feeling came over him. He felt silence coming from heaven. Stanley's words crowded his thoughts: *Maybe God's mad with you, if you didn't hear from him this morning. Sometimes my daddy just shuts up when he's sick of me.* Brother Moore honestly couldn't remember the last time he'd heard from God.

Suddenly, he caught a glimpse of himself rushing Mabel and the children this morning while he sipped coffee and read the paper. He peeked at Mabel in the choir stand. She looked so unhappy. Now that he thought about it, he hadn't seen her smile in a long time.

"Lord, what's happening to me?" he prayed. He waited, half expecting a verbal answer. But heaven's mouth was shut. Brother Moore began to sweat. He felt like God was ignoring him. For the first time, he felt how lonely it feels to be overlooked. Without words, he realized how he must look to God. *How must Mabel feel?* In a single moment, he realized that very few of his prayers probably were making it to heaven. He knew his life before God and before his family would have to change. For the first time in years, Brother Moore prayed from his heart: "Lord, have mercy...."

FOR FURTHER MEDITATION

Prayer

Dear Lord, my relationships with you and with my loved ones are precious to me. Whenever my prayers seem hindered, teach me to quickly examine my spiritual and earthly relationships. Draw me into a life of unbroken fellowship. Amen.

Day 29
Tough and Tender

"Here is my servant, whom I uphold, my chosen one in whom I delight; I will put my Spirit on him and he will bring justice to the nations. He will not shout or cry out, or raise his voice in the streets. A bruised reed he will not break, and a smoldering wick he will not snuff out. In faithfulness he will bring forth justice."

—Isaiah 42:1-3

Brothers, no one is more creative than us. Just think about it: our lives are dramas in action. "Hello" is insufficient. When we meet, hands slap, fists pound, thumbs lock, and fingers snap on the upswing. When we score in sports, the message is clear: for the moment, we are "The Man."

On the street we conjure images of superhuman feats. It seems we've had to create our own image of strength, because marginal history says that we have no "real power."

I began to think about manly strength after meeting a "tough" Native American brother from Seattle. From the beginning, I noticed something different about him. He greeted me with a simple, dare I say, tender handshake. He was soft-spoken, yet confident. He was self-assured, but his tenderness captured my attention. In a split second, I remembered: for Native Americans, shaking hands is a spiritual event. They believe that a harsh handshake will crush or bruise the spirit which is embraced in the process. "A bruised reed he will not break" (Isaiah 42:3a). Care marks the all-important moment of greeting. His tenderness stirred my soul to reflection.

How many spirits have I crushed through harsh words or actions? How many times do we brothers invite more trouble than it's worth by bellowing out demands and barking orders at loved ones?

"He will not shout or cry out, or raise his voice in the streets" (Isaiah 42:2).

Only the strong can be tender. Tenderness attracts good company. Compassion, respect, and admiration sit at its feet. When was the last time you were strong enough to be tender to your wife, children, or loved ones? People may think you're soft, but God knows you're strong.

With a prophetic message from God, Jesus was tough enough to face a sinful nation, yet he was tender in spirit. He wept over the death of Lazarus. With compassion, Jesus wept over crowds, healed the sick, and pitied the poor. He had an impact on people's lives because he allowed God to direct his life. Jesus courageously chose to be tough and tender. Being tender is a bold move, brother.

Are you tough enough?

FOR FURTHER MEDITATION

Prayer

My God, how complex I am! You have made me strong in body yet loving in heart. Help my words to be considerate when appropriate, and stern when necessary. I want to live as a complete man—courageous enough to be like Jesus. Amen.

The Next Step

1. Pray for God to work more tenderness into your conversations and actions.

2. Make an intentional effort to say or do something caring or tender to or for someone. Check your motives; share your tenderness without any notions of seducing or "getting over" on someone.

Day 30
The Other Woman

Husbands, love your wives, just as Christ loved the church and gave himself up for her.

—Ephesians 5:25

You'd better enjoy your last few days of quiet, Raymond. In a little while you won't remember silence, sleep, or your name—Daddy!"

Raymond's friends took their last verbal jabs at him before he left the bowling alley. Ray and his wife, Melba, were expecting their first child soon. The ultrasound had revealed that the baby was going to be a girl. For months, Ray had been gearing himself up for his first child. *I'm going to be the best daddy in the world. This child's going to get the best. I won't spoil her, though; she'll have to work hard. She'll learn how to dance, take music lessons, and run track, or whatever she wants to do.* Ray made and remade his mental checklist a thousand times.

When he got home that night, he found a note. Melba was at the hospital; her sister drove her there. Ray rushed to County General and raced to the receptionist's desk. Frantically, he asked, "Do you have a Melba Smothers here? She's having *my* baby!"

"Yes, sir, she's in room 405," came the calm reply.

Ray raced up the stairs; the elevator was too slow for him. Out of breath, he slid into the room, only to find an empty bed. "Nurse," Ray called as he reentered the hallway, "where's my wife? She's having *my* baby."

"Well," said the nurse, chuckling, "she's probably in delivery; that's where we deliver our babies around here. Why don't you go check in at the waiting room, and they'll keep you posted on her condition."

Ray was too nervous to catch her sarcasm. "Thanks," he said. In the waiting room Ray found Melba's sister, Corliss. "Did we have a baby yet?" Ray blurted.

"No, not yet. Melba's okay; they just took her in. It looks like the baby's coming any minute. We tried to call you, but the lines were all busy at the bowling alley."

Before she could tell Ray much more, the doctor came and asked for the Smothers family.

"Are you Mr. Smothers?" he asked Ray.

"Yes," Ray answered excitedly.

"Well, you have a fine baby girl. Congratulations!"

Ray went into orbit. "How many pounds is she? Does she have all her parts? When can I see her?"

The doctor answered each rapid-fire question. "By the way," said the doctor, "your wife's doing fine, if you want to see her for a few moments."

Ray half-heard the doctor's last comment. "Yeah, okay, but can I see my baby girl first right quick?"

That day, Ray took everyone to see *his* baby. It kind of got on Melba's nerves that Ray had held the baby before she did. When their pastor came to visit, he asked Melba what the baby's name was. Melba said half-jokingly, "I'm about ready to call her 'the other woman.' She's only been here a few hours and she's already got all of Ray's attention."

Two weeks after her birth, baby Jackie received a steady stream of visitors. Relatives and friends crowded around to see the first Smothers family grandchild. Ray gave everybody a blow-by-blow description of baby Jackie's first few days on earth. Melba did her best to smile and peek over everyone's shoulders to catch a glimpse of her baby. That evening, after everyone had gone, Melba started crying.

"Melba, what's wrong, baby?" Ray asked. "Something hurting you? Should I call the doctor?" He was puzzled

"No, Ray, you need a doctor, a psychologist," she replied. Then she started crying harder.

"Wait, baby, wait," Ray whispered. "Shhhhh…you're gonna wake up the baby."

"I don't care," Melba growled. "Ever since Jackie was born, you've treated me like I don't exist. Maybe I should just step to the side while you gloat over *your* baby."

For weeks, Melba had been silently suffering from the "baby blues," the depression that some women experience after their hormones skyrocket before birth and plunge after delivery. She was tired of still wearing her maternity clothes. Every time she wore them she wondered whether she'd ever get back into a size seven. Melba felt that she no longer mattered. People spoke to her as an aside: "Hi, Melba. Where's my baby?" Melba had had enough. This was her day, and she told the sky how she felt—about everything.

When she finished, Ray sat speechless. Melba threw her hands in the air. "So, you don't have anything to say? Fine! You and your woman can spend the rest of the night together." Melba walked out, slamming the front door behind her.

"Waaaaaa!" baby Jackie cried. Ray rushed over to the crib and picked her up.

"Shhhhh, Shhhhh, it's all right; Daddy's here." Ray rocked Jackie and thought about Melba. "Baby girl, we're in a mess. Mama says I'm spending so much time with you that I don't pay her any attention anymore. She calls you 'the other woman.'"

Ray paused and thought about it. "Maybe she's right. I never thought my own baby could come between me and my wife. You've got such cute squishy cheeks; who couldn't love such a pretty baby?" Ray swallowed hard and then made a confession. "I love you, baby Jackie, but you've got to be the baby, not 'the other woman.' I know you understand."

Baby Jackie cooed in his ear and then spit up all over his back. "So," Ray groaned, "you're not gonna take this lightly, are you?"

FOR FURTHER MEDITATION

Prayer

Dear Lord, there is nothing more important than sharing a caring, committed relationship. Help me to nurture the special relationship with the woman with whom I share my life.

The Next Step

1. "The other woman" comes in many forms, such as our
   a. children
   b. jobs
   c. hobbies
   d. friends (male or female)
Is there someone or something acting as "the other woman" in your life?

2. What things are you doing to ensure that the most important woman in your life is not competing with "the other woman"?

Day 31

You've Got to Love 'Em

Above all, love each other deeply, because love covers over a multitude of sins.

—1 Peter 4:8

Carlos, are those coals ready yet?" Denise asked.

Carlos and Denise always enjoyed the annual James family barbecue.

"Come on, Denise. Bring that meat over here and say 'have mercy,' because I'm gonna put a hurtin' on these ribs," Carlos said with a smile.

The savory aroma of hickory-smoked meat seemed to lure the rest of the relatives to the backyard. As usual, the teenagers huddled together, a party in the making. No one escaped their sharp eyes and quick comments.

"Hey, hey, look y'all," Douglas announced. "Here comes Aunt Luttie and Cousin 'T.' How long do you think it'll take before she goes into her act?"

Douglas started previewing "the act" in his best Aunt Luttie voice: "Tooooony! Bring me some more of that 'tata pie. But don't put no ice cream on it. I don't want my diabetes to act up."

Terrence interrupted, "Oh no! There's Uncle Milton. You think he knows what day it is yet? His eyes have that red glaze again. I hope he doesn't breathe over the barbecue—it'll light up like a torch."

Just then Sarita started giggling. "What's up, Rita?" the others asked.

"Check out Melvin's new girlfriend. She's got on so much makeup that her eyes can't even move. Somebody should have told her that you're supposed to take the mud pack off before you leave the beauty shop."

Denise walked over to the group with a perturbed look on her face. "Would you all help me out?" she whispered.

"What's up, Auntie?" they all chimed in. "Your Uncle Fred can't remember where he left his teeth again. He'll try to gum those rib bones if we don't help him."

"Aaaaaaaaah!" Aunt Luttie screamed as she pointed at her glass of lemonade.

"Luttie, Luttie, calm down, now. I thought that was my water glass," Uncle Fred pleaded. He had found his false teeth. The teenagers laughed until their insides hurt.

While they were settling down, Douglas whispered, "Uh oh, there's Drake. That brother is scary. He never says much, but he's always got on a bunch of gold jewelry. Everybody knows he doesn't work. I know he's our cousin, but I don't even know why he comes around here."

Carlos applied the last dabs of barbecue sauce on the ribs. With a satisfied grin on his face, he announced, "All right, we'll be ready to eat in a minute. Somebody find Uncle Milton and tell him to come on."

While the others gathered by the table, Carlos motioned to the teenagers to help him for a minute. He took the opportunity to drop some wisdom into their laps.

"You know," he began, "I've been listening to you this morning. Lighten up a little bit. Remember, we're all family. Everybody needs a place where they can feel safe and just be themselves—including Drake. Regardless of how ridiculous our folks may all look from time to time, you've still got to love 'em."

Jerome jumped to their defense. "Aw, Uncle Carlos, we were just having a little fun. Don't tell me you like everything our family does. Even the Bible says, God don't like ugly."

Carlos didn't miss a beat. "First of all, 'God don't like ugly' is not in the Bible. Second, God doesn't ask us to like everything that people do, but we do have to love everybody. You never know, your love may help some people straighten out their lives."

Denise eased over to where Carlos was standing. "Hey, sweetheart, what's up?" Carlos asked.

"Could you help me clean something up?" she said, gritting her teeth.

"What?" said Carlos, not really wanting to know. "It's Uncle Milton. Somehow he crawled into the backseat of your new car and left more than a memory on your upholstery."

"What!" Carlos exclaimed, dropping a burger into the white coals.

The teenagers eyed each other and said in unison, "Remember, you've got to love 'em."

FOR FURTHER MEDITATION

Prayer

Dear Lord, give me the extra strength and patience necessary to love my "difficult" family members. Amen.

Day 32

Precious Lord, Take My Hand

But Jesus knew what they were thinking and said to the man with the shriveled hand, "Get up and stand in front of everyone." So he got up and stood there.... He looked around at them all, and then said to the man, "Stretch out your hand." He did so, and his hand was completely restored.

—*Luke 6:8, 10*

No one knew why his hand was withered, shriveled, useless. Jewish culture surmised that sin caused sickness and poverty. People seem to enjoy concocting stories about how someone else acquired his or her dilemma. People gaze from inconspicuous distances to speculate on the *how's* and *why's*.

A voice in the crowd said, "Maybe he fell on it when he was young. You know young folks: no matter how much you warn them, they just have to do things their way. He probably was trying to touch something he had no business touching. A hard head makes a soft behind; looks like this time it made a withered hand."

A crude voice in the back whispered, "No, it's probably some disease. You know sickness runs in his family. His auntie, Mardell, tried to have children, and every one of them turned out strange. Those kids never had a chance with *them* as parents. Must be something in their genes."

"Perhaps it's deeper than that," uttered another knowledgeable soul. "Look at that hand. At times it seems full of self-pity. In other moments, it appears to glare at the world defiantly. Mostly it just waits, hoping to move again someday."

A resident mystic even claimed to be able to read the thoughts of that withered hand. He stood to give a first-hand report: "The withered hand holds nothing. Its strength shriveled. Fossil-like, its flexibility now stands frozen. I believe that this hand once held power and fame. Fortune and the future were never beyond his reach. Perhaps at one time he satisfied himself with what most men merely desire: to hold a good job, to capture the respect of others, to feel the soft touch of woman's companionship.

"These hands attracted no strange glance, until they started grabbing," the mystic continued. "If one was good, two were better. Big's too small; desire larger. Quick's no good; require faster. Success can ill afford contentment. Progress demands compulsion. He learned to seize, to hold, to hoard, to master. His life became mere grasping. He failed to see his friends retreat. They saw his soul-light fading.

"This hand withdrew from public view. He held his things and thoughts so close; his privacy was guarded. When others neared, his instinct changed his flesh to heartless steel. He closed his heart, his mind, himself. His vicelike grip held only domination. In time, this hand forgot to give. It only knew to take. His thoughts and things were now his own. His world became alone. He needs to be released from his own prison. His days are blurred emotions. He grieves this ostracized condition. He seethes in spite of his condition. He moans for someone to hear and care."

Finally, the mystic paused to consider his own wisdom.

In truth, only God knows why hands really wither. The cause may not be our concern. We all have withered hands. Someone or something may rob us of vitality. Some part of ourselves may feel shriveled. We may have held on to lifeless forms, only to be drained in the process. But God desires us to rise and be restored.

When Jesus opens withered hands, he releases new life that confounds critics and glorifies God. What would change if you dared to ask Jesus to restore what has withered in your life?

"Get up and stand in front of everyone . . ."
"Stretch out your hand."
He did so, and his hand was completely restored.
(Luke 6:8, 10)

FOR FURTHER MEDITATION

Prayer

Dear Lord, my vitality is withered. My resolve, my purpose, and my inspiration all need your refreshing touch. Renew my strength and confidence today. Breathe life into every part of me that lies shriveled. I can no longer waste my life. This is my time to stand and be healed. Amen.

Day 33
Brother Love

How good and pleasant it is when brothers live together in unity!

—*Psalm 133:1*

We love our mothers. We adore our wives. We cherish our children. But we need brothers. Not just blood brothers; we need men friends—brothers linked by a special bond of friendship.

"Brother love" forms in the crucible of hard times survived. "Brother love" emerges from the fires of adversity. Is there such a brother in your life? Someone who helped you when life seemed ready to crush your spirit? In the course of a lifetime, we may find one or two brothers with whom we dare to share our hearts. When this inseparable bond commences, no amount of time or distance can sever the relationship.

Some of us have friends living in cities thousands of miles away. Some of us have friends to whom we haven't spoken in a year or more. Yet when that moment arrives when we reconnect, it's as if it were old times again.

For several months, I observed a man serving overseas. His face seemed grim and worn. His eyes appeared unfamiliar with joy. The tedious routine of life gnawed at his motivation and drive. This was a man destined to sober existence—until he received some visitors. Some brothers came from across the waters to help him in a time of need. The help came in unconventional ways. They hunted together. They worked together. They joked and laughed together. They fellowshiped as only men can. "Brother love" massages pained hearts like no other love can. There's something about the camaraderie of brothers that brings out our best.

It really is good and pleasant when brothers live together in unity. Somehow "brother love" carries with it a strength for continuing the journey. "Brother love" brings new perspective to otherwise dismal situations. We all need brothers. They challenge us to greatness. They inspire us to dream again and try what we once abandoned.

When you think about it, "brother love" is a most powerful thing. Some of us live for years on the strength of a few brother-love encounters. "How good and pleasant it is when brothers live together in unity!"

FOR FURTHER MEDITATION

Prayer

Dear Lord, thank you for the brothers that you've brought into my life. I cherish those friendships now more than ever. Bless my brother-friends today. Amen.

The Next Step

1. If you have been out of contact with a brother-friend for sometime, why not call or write him today.

2. Make a point to keep in regular contact with the brothers who have helped nurture your life.

Day 34
Be 4 Real

Do not conform to the evil desires you had when you lived in ignorance. But just as he who called you is holy, so be holy in all you do.

—1 Peter 1:14-15

hone conversation:

How long has this been going on? Several years...oh, I see. And how did it start? You're not sure. Uh huh. One thing just led to another, and before you knew it, a wall stood between the two of you. What? Oh, you say it seems to be affecting your relationships with other people, too? Yeah, it happens like that. What's that? You say you think you feel worse than anybody else about it? Uh huh. Yep. Right, right. Yeah, those are the typical symptoms: irritable, easily angered, overly critical, troubled sleep, and difficulty concentrating. So what do you want me to do about this? Fix it? All right. It won't be easy, but I'll see what I can do.

Mr. Sorry hung up the phone, shaking his head. It had been a long week. This was his fourth call today. He'd heard from Mr. Baby Please, Mr. I'll Do Anything to Get You Back, and Mr. What Do You Want from Me. Sooner or later, they all come knocking on Mr. Sorry's door.

They all want some quick-fix solution for their problems. Even though it took them years to create the problem, they all expect Mr. Sorry to fix it in a moment's notice. If they only knew what it really takes to patch up a relationship. Sometimes, if they call right away, Mr. Sorry can rush right in and fix the problem. But most guys wait until the problem is so severe that the injured party doesn't want to hear anything that Mr. Sorry has to say.

This was a tough case. Mr. Sorry knew he would need help to fix this mess, so he decided to call his friends for some support. First he called Mr. Sweet Talk.

Mr. Sorry: Sugar Man, what's up, buddy? Look, I need a favor. You busy this evening? I need some backup. I've got a tough case over on First and Heartbreak Avenue.

Mr. Sweet Talk: Sorry, brother, I'm laying up here with a cast on my leg. You know, people just don't believe me like they used to. I used to walk up to women with some flowers, candy, and a card, say a few lines, and it was over. Now they tell me they've seen *Waiting to Exhale* and that I don't have what it takes. The last sister told me off so bad that I tripped down her back steps and broke my leg. Naw, Sorry, you better call for some heavy-duty backup.

Mr. Sorry hung up; he pulled out his phone book. *What can I do?* he thought to himself. *Let's see, who have I tried lately? Mr. Excuses—no, he's starting to repeat himself. Mr. Ignore the Problem—no, he never gets anything accomplished. Mr. Blame the Victim—no, he usually starts a bigger argument. Here we go . . .Mr. Big Stuff; he'll go with me.*

Mr. Sorry: Hey, Big Stuff, what's going on, man? Look, why don't you come make a run with me?

Mr. Big Stuff: I'm sorry, Sorry, Sugar Man just gave me the lowdown on your situation. Quiet as it's kept, people don't want a lot of stuff when they're angry. It almost seems to make things worse. I was over on Tempest Street the other day. I brought some of my best things: perfume, expensive dinner, new clothes, and a credit card. The sister told me, "Get with the times. I make more than you can bring, so do us both a favor and give your stuff to the poor and needy." Nobody takes me seriously anymore. Why don't you stop wasting your time with old news? Do yourself a favor and call Mr. Real.

Mr. Sorry thanked Big Stuff and thought about calling Mr. Real. The only problem is, Mr. Real is so expensive. Most guys don't want to pay what he charges. Mr. Sorry reflected on the last conversation he had had with Mr. Real.

Mr. Sorry: So, just what can my client expect from you? You know he's gonna ask.

Mr. Real: It's really simple. He's got to be completely honest with himself and with her. If he goes into the situation only to make himself look good, then he's lost already. He needs to honestly listen to what she has to say, and try to understand the situation from her perspective. Maybe if he learns what things are important to her, he won't trip all over her feelings next time. He's also got to be willing to honestly admit when he's wrong. The next part is hard for most brothers: he's got to honestly try to feel what she's feeling so he can be empathetic with her. If he learns to feel what she feels, he'll be able to understand her better.

Mr. Sorry: Okay, thanks for your help. I'll call my client and tell him what to expect.

Mr. Sorry thought about what Mr. Real had said. *You know, it doesn't seem like his demands are too much for a brother who really wants to keep his relationship together. But, that's something he'll have to decide. All I know is, Sorry ain't walkin' into that house alone. My mama didn't raise no fool.*

FOR FURTHER MEDITATION

Prayer

Dear God, many times I don't know what to say when there's a problem in my relationship with the woman I love. Part of me swells with pride, refusing to admit wrong. Another part of me wants pain-free reconciliation. Show me what to say and do to bring genuine healing and wholeness. Amen.

The Next Step

1. When do you usually call on Mr. Sorry? What do these situations have in common?

2. Is it difficult for you to tell your spouse or significant other when you are wrong?

3. The next time a difficulty arises in your dating, or marital relationship, ask yourself if saying "I'm sorry" is enough. Considering the inadequacy of merely saying "I'm sorry," what do you think is the best course of action to take?

Day 35

Stop the Battle Before It Begins

"In your anger do not sin": Do not let the sun go down while you are still angry.

—*Ephesians 4:26*

There is a silent killer running loose in our neighborhoods. His victims suffer various wounds: crushed spirits, broken hearts, bruised features, or bloodied bodies. This killer enters through the mind and exits through the mouth or the fist. The problem with this killer is his invisibility. He can strike anyone, anywhere, at any time. This enemy is uncontrolled anger.

We men never seem to escape the lure of anger. Perhaps the apostle Paul knew that completely avoiding anger is impossible. Life constantly provokes feelings of agitation and frustration. There are too many occasions for anger to surface.

There are just causes for which we should become angry: disrespect, discrimination, evil, corruption. These and other reasons can stir us to justified anger. Whether justified or not, the question is, what do we do with that anger? Do we allow it to have unlimited access to our minds?

Unchecked anger incubates seething, vengeful thoughts. The longer we allow anger to interpret life's events, the more likely we are to act in regrettable ways.

Anger can crowd out reason and sanity. Anger can push us to hasty decisions. Anger reacts to protect wounded egos and embarrassing shortcomings. Anger often hides from the truth.

Paul urges us to acknowledge our anger while simultaneously erecting barriers for containing it. "In your anger do not sin" (Ephesians 4:26). The spiritual man must learn to tie ropes of constraint on anger before he commits a worse deed.

Too many of us trespass into rage and foolishness. Our friends and families bear the scars. Muzzle your madness. Restrain your strength. Find safe places to vent. Talk it out. Run it off. Even though anger is inevitable, you can stop it from gaining destructive momentum.

Spiritual men know that no one can stop a righteous man from his destiny. Use that angry energy for some positive purpose. King was so angry that he marched for civil rights. Mandela was so upset that he endured years of imprisonment in order to free a nation. "Do not let the sun go down on your anger" (Ephesians 4:26 NRSV). Find a way to release and redirect that energy positively before the day passes.

God continues to uphold those who trust the Lord to provide solutions to wrongful deeds. Sometimes the greatest victories come when we choose not to act rashly. Many people simply fold when they see that nothing rattles you and causes unthinking retaliation. When you conquer anger, you stop the battle before it begins.

FOR FURTHER MEDITATION

Prayer

Dear God, when my blood boils with anger, give me restraint! Before I hurl insults or destroy friendships, teach me to pause. Before I succumb to an angry force greater than I am, help me to walk away. Before I create an ugly scene, where no one wins, remind me of what's really important. Deliver me from being enslaved by my own anger. Amen.

Spiritual Exercise

So many of us fall prey to destructive behaviors when we're angry. Why not choose to let your anger work for you in positive ways. Here are some suggestions for using the energy generated from anger:

1. Work it off through physical exercise.

2. Clean the garage, do some yard work, reorganize a storage room, and so forth.

3. Uncover all the issues by talking to someone; then begin working toward solutions.

4. Improve yourself: read, draw, play a musical instrument, barbecue, find a hobby.

Day 36
Making Waves

"Lord, if it's you," Peter replied, "tell me to come to you on the water." "Come," he said. Then Peter got down out of the boat, walked on the water and came toward Jesus.
—Matthew 14:28-29

Try it! Did someone you trust ever tell you that? Climb upon that bike and ride—try it! Work on your skills and go out for the basketball team—try it! Go to that big state university and study hard—try it! Many of us need someone to push us beyond what we think we're capable of doing.

Peter was willing to try. If anyone was to be involved with the daring and the novel, it was Peter. For a few exciting moments, Peter left the comfort of a boat that perhaps had sustained him along many a seagoing journey. Without hesitation, Peter found it more enticing to do the impossible with Jesus than to remain confined in status quo with his friends. For several glorious steps, Peter trusted in God more than in his own ability, logic, and reason. In every sense of the word, Peter was making waves.

Did you ever ask yourself why the other disciples remained on the boat? Too many of us do the same. Not only do we stay behind, but we also pull Peter's coat, trying to get him to stay with us. "Peter, are you crazy?" we say. "No one's ever done that before. Wait until the weather clears up so you can see what you're doing!" Instead of urging others on to greater faith, our human tendency is to destroy every new sprout of faith that emerges from someone else.

Every Peter who dares to climb out of the boat faces enormous pressure and expectation. First he must calm his own nerves. Then he must press past human objection and keep his eyes on Jesus long enough to accomplish the divine task. When the wind and waves kicked up, Peter lost his focus and began to sink. Although Jesus saved him immediately, he added a rebuke: "You of little faith...why did you doubt?" (Matthew 14:31*b*). It seems strange to chastise a man who just did what no one else had dared to do. Imagine what Jesus may have been thinking.

Perhaps Jesus was disappointed in the lost potential of that opportunity. What could have happened if Peter had completed his walk? Would the other disciples have been inspired to try? If Peter had succeeded, how many others would have found courage to trust God for greater things? When we dare to step out for Jesus, the Lord has expectations for us as well. The hope of other generations may rest upon us, too. Jackie Robinson tried. Tiger Woods tried. What would have happened if they had stopped? When God calls us to walk on water, it's a tall order for us and countless others. Take the invitation seriously.

The next time you face the impossible, ask the Lord if you are to walk ahead. If God calls you forth, don't be afraid. This is your time to make a big splash for the Lord.

FOR FURTHER MEDITATION

Prayer

Dear Lord, facing the impossible demands deep faith in you. Teach me to trust your invitations. With you, all things are possible. Give me the courage to walk on the water. Only you know how my act of faith may benefit future generations. Amen.

Spiritual Exercise

Have you been balking at some recent invitation to "walk on the water"? Commit the issue to God in prayer and actively listen for the Holy Spirit to call you forth.

Day 37

Male by Birth, Man by Choice

When I was a child, I talked like a child, I thought like a child, I reasoned like a child. When I became a man, I put childish ways behind me.

—1 Corinthians 13:11

Want to start an interesting conversation? Then ask the average brother this question: What makes a man a man?

Don't be surprised by the wide variety of replies you get. No one seems to know exactly what the answer is these days. Confused youth think manhood means making babies, living above the law, or smoking more dope than anyone else. Unthinking souls play the numbers game: "I'm a man when I'm sixteen and can drive," or "when I'm eighteen and can vote," or "when I'm old enough to buy liquor legally." Older brothers boast of holding a good job, raising a family, and commanding respect.

Consider our African heritage. There was a time when we had adult rites of passage. Men took boys through teachings and rituals to prepare them for manhood. Men challenged boyish conduct and character through tests of achievement, decision making, and morality. Manhood was not a given; it was a conscious choice, a true sacrifice, a noble honor. Today, there are still some African cultures in which men remain boys if they fail to complete their adult rites of passage. Unfortunately, there are too many "uninitiated" boys in our communities. They're not men; they are confused imitations.

Do you recall your journey into manhood? When did *you* realize that you were a man? When did *others* recognize that you were a man? Can you remember the bridge that brought you from boyhood to manhood? What did it require of you? What decisions confronted you? How did you change? Becoming a man is a process, not a single act in time. The major factor that determines manhood is choice.

We must choose to be men. By definition, we must put away childish behaviors and attitudes. People must be able to see a distinction between the way we once acted and the way we now conduct ourselves. Manhood is an evolution. In our society, the need for men—Black men—is enormous.

Paul recognized that his declaration of manhood was a line of demarcation. It was a time to grow up. He changed his speech. He changed his reasoning. Last, he put childish ways behind him. His family, his society, and his spiritual zeal provoked him to leave boyhood behind. Paul made a conscious choice to be a man. You must walk down a similar path.

There is one final note of consideration. You've got to see a man in order to be a man. Look to Jesus, the only perfect example. Jesus represents the truth that manhood cannot be fully achieved without developing one's self spiritually. Spiritual men are brave enough to submit their egos to God, their wills to the Holy Spirit, and their lives to the Lord. Only Jesus can lead us into the kind of manhood that we'll need in order to successfully maneuver through the maze of life. So many brothers are content to be somebody's baby; why don't you decide to be a man by choice?

FOR FURTHER MEDITATION

Prayer

Dear Lord, I must be a man in your eyes. Challenge my childish ways. Lead me to deeper spirituality. Build in me an immovable faith and integrity. I choose to walk with you as a man in every sense of the word. Amen.

The Next Step

Becoming a strong well-rounded man is a lifelong effort. Consult the Suggested Reading List for areas in which you would like to develop yourself—culturally and spiritually. Challenge yourself to read constantly and to learn.

Day 38
Who I Am!

Therefore, if anyone is in Christ, he is a new creation; the old has gone, the new has come!
                                        —*2 Corinthians 5:17*

I wish I knew...
        oh, how I want to know...
                who I am.
Too many voices volunteer my answer for me.

After being dumped in this distant land,
I was free labor,
        cheap sport,
            an endless point of ridicule.
When my useful days did cease, they declared me
invisible.

Am I "Invisible Man"?
Every day I see my substance,
        flesh and bone,
                face and physique,
                    but society overlooks me.
The laws ignore my existence
        and only feign response when I protest or riot.

Can you hear an Invisible shout?
　　　No!
Only when they feel an Invisible slap
　　　do they sense my presence.
Must I exist only in rebellion?

Is that who I am, a reaction?
I rebel in retaliation
　　　against every expert who declares me a problem.
How does it feel to be a problem?
　　　If a problem I am,
　　　then I must find my solution.
I'm smart, you know.
　　　I found a clue.
　　　　　　I learned the game.
　　　　　　　　I play the role.

Every day I wear the mask of expectation.
　　　I am more or less what I need to be.
　　　　　　No one knows who I really am...
　　　　　　　　not even me.

I lost myself to play this part.
　　　I drained my living emotion.
　　　　　　My skin lost its body heat—
　　　　　　I'm cool.

I'm cool in the midday sun.
　　　I walk while others run.
　　　　　　I know when others wonder.
I don't surprise;
　　　I watch behind.
　　　　　　Some merely think;
　　　　　　I strategize
In hopes that one day too
　　　I'll rise...

I bought a suit and went uptown to be a true success.
　　I schooled my mind and
　　　　groomed my manners.
　　　　　　I spoke as others speak.

I climbed the corporate ladder and lunched with *him*.
　　I chased success with every whim.
　　　　I knew the next advance was mine.
Then his nephew jumped in line.
　　I walked away when I realized.
　　　　I was an almost was...

Who am I?

My soul is weary, near collapse.
　　This life extracts a heavy tax.
Where can I find my soul's relief?
　　Who knows my inward groan and grief?

　*I lift up my eyes to the hills—where does my help come
from? My help comes from the LORD, the Maker of heaven
and earth.*

　　　　　　　　　　　　　　(Psalm 121:1-2)

I speak to God and learn what's true.
　　God has my soul and now I'm new.
Go, cruel voices from the past;
　　You won't control my future.
My promise is divine in root.
　　I now know who I am.

I am the one who becomes.

I am God's handiwork,
　　　　a miracle in motion.
　　　　　　I am a son of God.
That is who I am.

131

Prayer

Dear Lord, free me from the stereotypes of the past. Reveal the man whom you created me to be. Let me live in the freedom of your definition for my life. Amen.

Day 39

If You Could Start All Over Again . . .

Do you not know that your body is a temple of the Holy Spirit, who is in you, whom you have received from God? You are not your own.

—*1 Corinthians 6:19*

riving in downtown traffic was always tedious. Chester hardly noticed the road signs and buildings anymore. They had become all-too-familiar landmarks along an unchanging path. Only the company of a local FM station eased the monotony of his early-morning travel. The voice of the radio announcer lured Chester's attention to the live interview of a jazz saxophone player. A personal collection of John Coltrane, Charlie "Bird" Parker, Dexter Gordon, and others attested to Chester's interest in the topic.

Soon Chester became oblivious to the outside world, thoroughly immersed in the unfolding story of how this jazz great reached the top. Chester hoped there would be something said in this interview that might serve as inspiration for his life. In the next moment, the interviewer asked a question that demanded considerable deliberation: "If you could start all over again, what would you do differently?" Chester leaned forward in anticipation of some deep philosophical answer. Surely this was the moment of inspiration he was waiting for. The reply came housed in a simple, yet profound, statement.

"Well," began the husky-voiced veteran, "if I started all over again, I'd take better care of my teeth. I'm fifty-six years old, with fifteen or twenty good playing years ahead of me. I could face them better if I hadn't been negligent with my health."

Why is it that we brothers too often forget that our bodies need regular care and attention? It's a well-known fact that many of us don't live long enough to collect a single Social Security check. We suffer. Our wives suffer. Our children wonder why we die so soon. God also stands in that line of mourners with a particular concern. Our bodies are not our own; they are the temples of the Holy Spirit.

God has expectations and hopes for these earthen vessels. All too often our vitamin-deficient, disease-ridden, sorely abused bodies fall across death's doorstep and look up at Jesus with a sheepish look of embarrassment.

Chester began to reexamine the way he was treating his body. *Maybe it's time for me to take my health a little more seriously*, he thought.

Maybe you and I should, too. Why not do something really spiritual today: get a physical, improve your diet, and exercise regularly. After all, your body belongs to God.

FOR FURTHER MEDITATION

Prayer

Dear Lord, I realize that my health is not my concern alone. To be healthy is to respect the body that you gave me. Good health is also a blessing to those who love me and depend on me. Today I pledge to be more conscientious about preserving my health. Amen.

The Next Step

1. Many of the illnesses we face are hereditary. Take time to speak to family members to determine the kinds of physical problems that are specific to your family. Afterward, devise a plan to counteract any potential health threats.

2. Many physical illnesses begin when we allow unresolved mental concerns to linger unaddressed: anger, worry, doubts, and so forth. These types of issues can and should be the regular topic of prayer and conversation with a trusted friend or loved one. How often do you address your problems through active prayer and dialogue with others?

Day 40
Till We Meet Again

Brothers, we do not want you to be ignorant about those who fall asleep, or to grieve like the rest of men, who have no hope. We believe that Jesus died and rose again and so we believe that God will bring with Jesus those who have fallen asleep in him.

—1 Thessalonians 4:13-14

I never thought it would come to this," Henry sighed to himself. His eyes wandered aimlessly about his shriveled, fifty-three-year-old body. Henry's family huddled closely around his hospital bed, not knowing what to say. Years of hard factory work had taken its toll on his once virile body. Decades of exposure to aluminum dust and other chemicals had reduced him to a mass of perishing flesh.

Henry Clavon was a good husband, a patient father, and a man who trusted God. It seemed so cruel that now his life was fading. Just a month ago, he and his wife, Margaret, started dreaming about their retirement. In five years, Henry could attend the thirty-year retirement party and collect his company pin. Margaret moved close to her husband of twenty-two years and gently kissed his hand.

"Hank, we're still praying for you. Don't give up," she said. But in her heart she knew his time was short. *Lord,* she prayed silently, *if he must go, take him gently; don't let him suffer.*

"Daddy?"

Sharon, their twenty-year-old daughter had rushed home from college to see him. "Daddy...oh, daddy," she whispered. Her body hung limp around her frame. Despair smothered the rest of her words. She had never seen her father so sick.

Henry reached up slowly and stroked her face with the edge of his index finger. "Punkin," he said, "you watch after your mama for me. You know she likes to know that you're all right. She's more than your mama now; she's your friend, too. You can trust her because she knows you and she loves you."

Sharon barely managed a "Yes, Daddy" before choking back more tears.

Eighteen-year-old Richard took it the hardest. He and his father had had their differences over the years. "Dad, I...I don't know what to say," he said as his mind flooded with the poison of past memories. *Too many arguments*, Richard thought. *They all seem so futile now.* As he stood on the threshold of manhood, he was beginning to realize just how much he needed a father.

"Dad, I just want to say...I'm sorry we never got it together. I mean, I don't know why I was always arguing with you."

Henry's cheeks picked up the corners of his mouth, forming a weak smile. "You're no different than I was. My dad almost put me out because of my mouth. I had to take a long, hard look at myself one day. Finally I realized that all that arguing wasn't doing any good. I decided I was more intelligent than that. And I just stopped fighting with him. We could talk then. Your grandfather never gave up on me...and I've never given up on you."

Lord, Henry prayed, *you're gonna have to help Ricky on the rest of his journey. Jesus, show him what it means to be a man.*

Just then the doctor came in. "Mrs. Clavon," he said, "may I speak with you a moment?"

Henry pulled himself up onto one side. "Wait a minute, Doc. I'm the patient, and this is my family. Whatever you've got to say, say it so we can all hear it together."

"All right," answered Dr. Henderson soberly. He breathed in and pushed out these words: "You have an acute case of the most aggressive cancer that there is. It has spread throughout 80 percent of your body. You may have only two weeks to live." Henry nodded without saying anything. Margaret asked Dr. Henderson about hospice care, and thanked him for being honest with them.

After Dr. Henderson left, Henry called for his family to come near him. "You all know I love you. Me and your mama have a will and burial insurance, so don't worry about any of that."

Henry told them how proud he was of them, until the sedative coaxed his eyes to sleep. Margaret and the children held Henry's hands. They shared the Twenty-third Psalm and prayed the Lord's Prayer together. Without prompting, Richard started singing, "Till we meet, till we meet, till we meet at Jesus' feet...."

The others joined in: "God be with you till we meet again."

As they sang with trembling voices, Henry's eyes fluttered opened, his lips parted into a smile, and he breathed his last breath. His family sensed that Henry had prepared to die. He'd made his peace with God. He'd made his peace with his family, and he'd paved the way for them to meet again.

FOR FURTHER MEDITATION

Prayer

Dear God, show me how to make my peace with you and my family early in life. Help me to live in such a way that I can face death with no regrets. Amen.

The Next Step

1. Do you have a legal will?

2. Do you have sufficient life insurance to insure your family's well-being in the event that you may die prematurely?

3. Are you participating in any investment program to supplement your income in your later years?

4. If you need to address any of the above three issues, make plans to actively deal with them immediately.

5. Take time to assess your relationship with your family. Are there things you need to be sure to tell them?

6. How is your relationship with Jesus Christ? Now is the time to commit your life to him.

Suggested Reading List

Professional athletes train. Outstanding musicians practice. Great men read. There is nothing like a "stretching" experience to stimulate growth and maturity. This suggested reading list is meant to provide such an opportunity. Each selection offers helpful insights into crucial issues for African American men. Discovering manhood is the journey of a lifetime. Only those who prepare themselves well can expect to cope with life's unique challenges. Read, reflect, and learn. This is the next step of the journey.

ON GAINING BETTER UNDERSTANDING OF BLACK WOMEN

Carter, Norvella, and Matthew Parker, eds. *Women to Women: Perspectives of Fourteen African-American Christian Women*. Grand Rapids, Michigan: Zondervan, 1996.

Collins, Patricia Hill. *Black Feminist Thought: Knowledge, Consciousness, and the Politics of Empowerment*. New York: Routledge, 1990.

Giddings, Paula. *When and Where I Enter: The Impact of Black Women on Race and Sex in America*. New York: Bantam Books, 1984.

Hicks, Ingrid D. *For Black Women Only: A Complete Guide*

to a Successful Life-Style Change, Health, Wealth, Love, and Happiness. Chicago: African American Images, 1991.

Hollies, Linda H. *Inner Healing for Broken Vessels: Seven Steps to a Woman's Way of Healing*. Nashville: Upper Room Books, 1992.

Hooks, Bell. *Ain't I a Woman? Black Women and Feminism*. Boston: South End Press, 1981.

White, Evelyn C. *Chain Chain Change: For Black Women Dealing with Physical and Emotional Abuse*. Seattle: The Seal Press, 1985.

————, ed. *The Black Women's Health Book: Speaking for Ourselves*. Seattle: The Seal Press, 1990.

ON DEVELOPING GREATER AWARENESS OF BLACK MANHOOD ISSUES

Akbar, Na'im. *Chains and Images of Psychological Slavery*. Jersey City, N.J.: New Mind Productions, 1984.

Asante, Molefi K. *The Afrocentric Idea*. Philadelphia: Temple University Press, 1988.

————. *Afrocentricity: The Theory of Social Change*. Trenton, N.J.: Africa World Press, 1990.

Hutchinson, Earl Ofari. *Black Fatherhood: The Guide to Male Parenting*. Los Angeles: Middle Passage Press, 1995.

————. *Black Fatherhood II: Black Women Talk About Their Men*. Los Angeles: Middle Passage Press, 1994.

————. *The Assassination of the Black Male Image*. Los Angeles: Middle Passage Press, 1994.

June, Lee N., ed. *The Black Family: Past, Present, and Future*. Grand Rapids, Mich.: Zondervan, 1991.

————, and Matthew Parker., eds. *Men to Men: Perspectives of Sixteen African-American Christian Men*. Grand Rapids, Mich.: Zondervan, 1996.

Karenga, Maulana. *Introduction to Black Studies*. Los Angeles: University of Sankore Press, 1982.

Kunjufu, Jawanza. *Developing Positive Self-Images and Discipline in Black Children*. Chicago: African American Images, 1984.

———. *Critical Issues in Educating African American Youth: A Talk with Jawanza*. Chicago: African American Images, 1989.

———. *Black Economics: Solutions for Economic and Community Empowerment*. Chicago: African American Images, 1991.

Lane, Eddie B. *Parenting: In the Context of a Spiritual Deficit*. Dallas: Black Family Press, 1997.

Lindsay, Jeanne Warren. *Coping with Reality: Dealing with Money, In-Laws, Babies and Other Details of Daily Life*. Buena Park, Calif.: Morning Glory Press, 1995. (Curriculum Guide and Student Workbook/Study Guide also available.)

Madhubuti, Haki. *Black Men: Obsolete, Single, Dangerous? Essays in Discovery, Solution, and Hope*. Chicago: Third World Press, 1990.

Nix, Sheldon D., Ph.D. *Becoming Effective Fathers and Mentors (A Guide to Prepare Men for the Task of Mentoring African American Boys)*. Colorado Springs, Colo.: Cook Communications Ministries, 1996.

———. *Let the Journey Begin (A Comprehensive Curriculum for Leading African American Boys Down the Road to Manhood)*. Colorado Springs, Colo.: David C. Cook Publishing Co., and Woodbury, N.J.: Renaissance Productions, 1996.

———. *Let the Journey Begin (Boy's Activity Book)*. Colorado Springs, Colo: Cook Communications Ministries, and Woodbury, N.J.: Renaissance Productions, 1996.

Reed, James W. *The Black Man's Guide to Good Health*. New York: Perigee Books, 1994.

Rogers, J.A. *World's Great Men of Color*. Vols. 1 and 2. New York: Collier Books, 1972.

Stephens, Brooke, ed. *Men We Cherish: African-American Women Praise the Men in Their Lives*. New York: Anchor, 1997.

T'Shaka, Oba. *The Art of Leadership*. Vol. 1. Richmond, Calif.: Pan Afrikan Publications, 1989.

———. *The Art of Leadership*. Vol. 2. Richmond, Calif.: Pan Afrikan Publications, 1991.

Wade-Gayles, Gloria., ed. *Father Songs: Testimonies by African-American Sons and Daughters*. Boston: Beacon Press, 1997.

Willis, Andre C., ed. *Faith of Our Fathers (African-American Men Reflect on Fatherhood*. With essays by Henry Louis Gates, Jr., Cornel West, John Edgar Wideman, Charles Ogletree, and eight others. New York, N.Y.: Penguin Group, 1996.

ON DEVELOPING OUR SPIRITUAL SELVES

Bailey, Randall C., and Jacquelyn Grant., eds. *The Recovery of Black Presence: An Interdisciplinary Exploration*. Nashville: Abingdon Press, 1995.

Blackwell, Luther. *The Heritage of the Black Believer (Discovering the Richness of the Black Man's Contribution to the Church)*. Shippensburg, Pa.: Treasure House, 1993.

Felder, Cain H. *Troubling Biblical Waters*. Maryknoll: Orbis, 1989.

———, ed. *The Original African-American Heritage Study Bible*. Nashville: James C. Winston, 1993.

———. *Stony the Road We Trod*. Minneapolis: Fortress, 1991.

Fosua, A. Safiyah. *Mother Wit: 365 Meditations for African-American Women*. Nashville: Abingdon Press, 1996.

Kunjufu, Jawanza. *Adam! Where Are You? Why Most Black Men Don't Go to Church*. Chicago: African American Images, 1994.

Lincoln, C. E., and L. H. Mamiya. *The Black Church in the African American Experience*. Durham, N.C.: Duke University Press, 1990.

McCray, Walter A. *The Black Presence in the Bible*. Vol. 1. Chicago: Black Light Fellowship, 1990.

———. *The Black Presence in the Bible and the Table of Nations*. Vol. 2. Chicago: Black Light Fellowship, 1990.

McKissic, William D., Sr. *Beyond Roots II: If Anybody Ask You Who I Am (A Deeper Look at Blacks in the Bible)*. Wenonah, N.J.: Renaissance Productions, 1994.

Paris, Peter J. *The Spirituality of African Peoples: The Search for a Common Moral Discourse*. Minneapolis: Fortress Press, 1995.

Waters, Kenneth L., Sr. *Afrocentric Sermons: The Beauty of Blackness in the Bible*. Valley Forge: Judson Press, 1993.

Weems, Renita J. *Just a Sister Away: A Womanist Vision of Women's Relationships in the Bible*. San Diego, Calif.: LuraMedia, 1988.

———. *I Asked for Intimacy: Stories of Blessings, Betrayals, and Birthings*. San Diego, Calif.: LuraMedia.

Wright, Jeremiah A., Jr., and Jini Kilgore Ross, ed. *What Makes You So Strong? Sermons of Joy and Strength*. Valley Forge: Judson Press, 1993.

———, and Colleen Birchett, ed. *Africans Who Shaped Our Faith: A Study of 10 Biblical Personalities*. Chicago: Urban Ministries, 1995.